CARY GRANT: TAKING THE LEAD

By Gene Popa

CARY GRANT: TAKING THE LEAD
By Gene Popa
Copyright © 2022 Gene Popa
No part of this book may be reproduced in any form or by any means, electronic, mechanical, digital, photocopying, or recording, except for inclusion of a review, without permission in writing from the publisher or Author.
No copyright is claimed for the photos within this book. They are used for the purposes of publicity only.

Published in the USA by:
BearManor Media
1317 Edgewater Dr #110
Orlando, FL 32804
www.bearmanormedia.com

Perfect ISBN 978-1-62933-961-0
Case ISBN 978-1-62933-962-7
BearManor Media, Orlando, Florida
Printed in the United States of America
Book design by Robbie Adkins, www.adkinsconsult.com

-TABLE OF CONTENTS-

Introduction v
-1- 1904 -1931. 1
-2- 1932 -1936. 18
-3- 1937 29
-4- 1938 66
Photo Gallery. 90
-5- 1939 118
-6- 1940 147
FREELANCE FILMS 1937-1940. 173
Radio Appearances 1937-1940 184
Index 186

For Dahlia, with whom every day's a holiday.

-INTRODUCTION-

"Everyone wants to be Cary Grant. Even I want to be Cary Grant."

When Cary Grant died on November the 29th of 1986, it was front page news around the world. This for an actor who had voluntarily left filmmaking behind him twenty years previous and retreated from the celebrity spotlight.

Earlier that same year, another actor named Brian Aherne had also passed away. There were some parallels in the lives of Aherne and Grant; both were born in England, each got their starts as actors on the stage, both made their American film debuts for Paramount Pictures in the early 1930s, and both were leading men right from the start. Unlike Grant, who had signed a long-term contract with Paramount, Aherne preferred to remain a freelance actor, alternating between films for various Hollywood (and British) studios and returning to Broadway.

Aherne starred in a number of notable films in the 1930s, including *The Song of Songs* (1933) with Marlene Dietrich, *What Every Woman Knows* (1934) with Helen Hayes, *I Live My Life* (1935) with Joan Crawford, and *Sylvia Scarlett* (1935) with Katharine Hepburn… and Cary Grant. In 1940 he earned a Best Supporting Academy Award nomination. He was, by any estimation, a movie star.

Yet upon his death in 1986, his passing was only briefly noted by the press. Citing this is not meant to disparage Mr. Aherne, but rather to illustrate how Cary Grant had elevated himself from being a "mere" movie star in Hollywood's so-called 'Golden Age', and had transformed himself into a cultural idol, retaining that iconic status decades after he put acting behind him.

In describing Grant, the journalists used words like *style*, *elegance*, *wit*, *charm*, and most of all, *legend*. While all of that absolutely applied, few noted the qualities that made him a legend: *resolve, nerve, intellect*.

For Cary Grant didn't just become legendary by happenstance; he took tremendous career risks to make it happen. If all it took to be a timeless celebrity icon were good looks, luck, hard work, and yes talent, then Brian Aherne and a thousand other leading men from the Thirties would have remained every bit as famous as Grant for the rest of their lives and beyond.

However, it took all of that and more. It took jeopardizing everything he had gained, even knowing the odds were powerfully against him. Cary Grant took that risk, and because of that to this day, nearing forty years after his demise, he remains for millions of people the world over the standard by which we measure style, elegance, wit and charm.

After reading this book, I hope you also apply him as a measure for resolve, nerve and intellect. For that is what took him from being a movie star and made him a legend.

That's what made him Cary Grant.

=1=
1904 - 1931

In August of 1931, things everywhere had gone from bad to worse. The Wall Street crash of 1929, which triggered a spiraling financial recession, had by this time become a full-fledged depression. That summer, thousands of banks across the United States, including major institutions in New York and Chicago, teetered on the brink of collapse, and hundreds shuttered their doors completely. Major banks in Germany, Austria and other European nations collapsed, and Great Britain tried to salvage the tumbling value of the pound by going off of the gold standard, resulting in a subsequent run by European financial houses on U.S. gold reserves that undermined the solvency of the American dollar and played further havoc with the economy. The consequences saw the savings of many wiped out virtually overnight.

The average American was bringing home about $25 in wages each week. That is, if they were still lucky enough to be employed. By year's end, the unemployment rate would be nearly 16% nationwide, and charity soup kitchens were common sights in cities and towns from coast to coast.

All of which made it a risky venture to voluntarily leave a job with no guarantee of finding other employment anytime soon. And it seemed the peak of outright insanity to give up a job that paid a princely $300 a week!

Yet that is precisely what Archie Leach had resolved to do.

It was by no means some spontaneous lark on his part. While his actions often did seem to some to be impulsive, they were in fact almost always the result of considerable quiet contemplation on his part. Archie may not have been a man with a grand plan for his life, but he was always at least thinking about what his next move should be.

While at first glance it may have seemed foolish for him to give up what he had, he knew full well that what he had held no guarantees. And it was by no means the first time he had leapt from the familiar and flung himself into the unknown. Nor would it be the last.

Archibald Alec Leach was born in Bristol, England on January 18th of 1904 to Elias and Elsie Leach. His father was a presser at a clothing factory, which provided steady work but only modest wages. The Leach's first child, John, had died in February of 1900, just two days shy of his first birthday, from tuberculous meningitis, and Elsie in particular took his death hard, sinking into what would now be considered a deep clinical depression. When Archie was born, she doted on him around the clock, determined to keep him healthy and safe, and did not relent in her attentions as her baby grew into childhood. Elias felt she was smothering their son and not allowing him to enjoy the kind of youthful experiences other boys his age did, but Elsie steadfastly continued to focus all of her attention on Archie, and kept him close to her as much as possible. But what made the relationship between mother and child a difficult one for the growing boy was that Elsie was not demonstrative with her affection, so for all of her overwhelming presence in his daily life, he rarely experienced what one would characterize as motherly love from her.

Many years later, the reflective son observed, "She wanted control of me because she couldn't control what had happened to her first son."

The marital relationship between Elsie and Elias had also grown brittle, to the point where after work, rather than return home, he would spend most evenings in pubs, and subsequently developed issues with alcoholism. When Elias was in the home, husband and wife would either argue, or else engage in extended spells of non-communication. All of this young Archie unhappily observed, and it skewed his understanding of relations between men and women for years to come.

As difficult as his relationship with his mother was, it at least provided a type of stability for him. All of that was swept away when he came home from school one day, only to find his mother wasn't there, but with his father waiting for him. Elias quietly explained to his nine-year-old son that his mother's nerves had become taxed, and so she was taking an extended holiday out of town to regain her health. In fact, Elias had committed her to a mental hospital.

Elsie Leach's behavior had grown steadily more erratic since the death of her first born, and in recent months she had begun to suffer from what appeared to be a sharpening emotional breakdown; she would speak nonsensically to no one in particular, she became obsessive compulsive, and would go into what appeared to be trances, drifting deep within her own mind, oblivious to the outer world. The family's doctor recommended she be institutionalized for treatment.

Archie learned to adapt to his new situation as best he could. Son and father had a detached relationship, after years of Elsie placing herself between them, and her absence now did little to bridge the gap between them. His father's drinking had not abated, so it was often left up to Archie to tend to himself, including making meals and tidying up.

Then came the day Elias informed his son, without any further explanation, that his mother had died. Not long after, Elias "married" again. In fact, he remained wed to Elsie, as he could not legally divorce her so long as she was in the sanitarium. Instead, he took a common law wife, Mabel Johnson Bass. She had scant interest in raising Elsie's son, and indeed soon enough became pregnant herself, giving birth to a boy she and Elias named Eric. Archie more or less became a boarder in his own home, rather than a member of the family.

However, in many ways this was nevertheless a happy time for Archie. Never a bad student, he began taking even more interest in his studies, and earned a place at Fairfield Secondary, an excellent school. He developed a liking for sports and discovered a natural athletic ability. He joined the Boy Scouts. He had a bright and breezy personality, and drew a wide circle of friends to himself. And while his relationship with his father was little more than formally correct, he developed an appreciation for dressing well from Elias, who because of his work in the garment industry had a keen eye for stylish clothing. This trait would serve his son well in the years to come.

Bristol, one of England's largest cities, was a thriving seaport, and the 19th Century had seen a flourishing of factories as well, but in certain respects the city's better days were behind it, with fewer and fewer economic opportunities for someone of limited means to rise above their station. Additionally, there was Britain's rigid class system, which did little to encourage the common people to elevate their place in life. Entering his teenage years, Archie began to consider his future prospects, and was unenthusiastic about them.

He could be a merchant sailor, or work on the docks, or find a position in a factory or as a shop clerk, but none of those possibilities interested him much. While he didn't consider manual labor beneath him, neither did Archie want to spend his life slaving away in a workshop or a shipyard for meager wages. Yet, he didn't actually know what else he wanted to do for a career.

Another option for young men looking to improve their station was the military. During the Great War, Archie volunteered as a messenger down on the docks, and seeing shattered soldiers brought back from France on stretchers convinced him that a future in khaki was not for him.

He had displayed an affinity for his chemistry classes, and was entertaining the notion of apprenticing in a technical trade. That was the sort of job that he could take anywhere in Britain, or the world. It wasn't glamourous, but it could provide steady employment.

As fate would have it, a science teacher at Fairfield did electrical work outside of the school, and he had recently helped install a new electrical system in the Bristol Hippodrome. Thinking that being an electrician might appeal to his career-minded student, he asked Archie if he would like to accompany him to the theatre during a Saturday matinee, so that he could see the system in use. There's no account of young Archie ever having expressed much interest in the live theatre before then, and although he had always enjoyed going to the movies (particularly to see the comedies of Charlie Chaplin), he had never evidenced much awareness of the British music hall.

The Hippodrome was one of the grand theatrical palaces that were blossoming across Great Britain in the early 20th Century. Ornately decorated, with a large dome overhead, it seated nearly 2,000 patrons. Its unique feature was a water tank adjacent to the stage which could hold 10,000 gallons, allowing the theatre to simulate rain, a waterfall or a river, should the production require it.

Everything from the hydraulics for the water tank to the stage lighting was state of the art for the era, and an electrician's dream to study. As he stood in the wings, Archie's attention was fixated not on the technical wonders of the Hippodrome, but rather the performances unfolding on the stage. Just as exciting was the bustling activity backstage. "I found myself in a dazzling land of smiling, jostling people," he later said. "They were wearing all sorts of costumes and doing all sorts of clever things. And that's when I knew. What other life could there be?"

As the show came to an end and the curtain closed, Archie Leach understood one thing above all others: a life on the stage could be the only future for him.

He began hanging around backstage at the Hippodrome, as well as another music hall, the Empire, where he eventually got himself hired as an assistant lighting worker. That lasted only until Archie, enthralled by the act of a stage magician, allowed his spotlight to drift off the performer and expose to the audience the mirrors used to create his illusions. Later in his life, when in interviews he would often tell fabulist tales of his youth, Cary Grant would chuckle and say that his blunder got him bounced right out of the Empire. Yet in fact he wasn't fired, but instead was reassigned as a backstage "gofer," carrying messages and running errands for the performers and crew. He actually found this more enjoyable than sitting up in the catwalk aiming a light, because now he was in the thick of the goings on, sharing in the conviviality and experiencing some of the sorely desired attentiveness he lacked at home.

Eventually he managed to get hired on in a similar role at the Hippodrome, but as his work, as well as his relationships with the many dancers, musicians, comics and acrobats broadened, his schoolwork began to suffer. His grades fell, he began skipping classes, and when he was in attendance, he often pulled pranks and caused mischief for his instructors. By some accounts, Archie was intentionally trying to get himself expelled, so that he could then join a traveling troupe of tumblers he had met at the Hippodrome. More than likely, he simply lost interest in schooling because he was bedazzled by the music hall. Whatever the reason, he in fact was expelled from Fairfield, and in true showman's style: he was called to the front of the hall during an assembly of the entire student body, and then after the list of his myriad transgressions was read aloud, he was commanded to leave, and never darken the school's doorway again. Archie was mortified, but quickly enough saw the episode as an opportunity. If he was indeed going to pursue a career as a performer, then now was the time to start.

As far as he was concerned, that career would begin with the Pender Troupe. Headed by Bob Pender (born Robert Lomas) and his wife Margaret, the troupe was well-established throughout the British entertainment circuit as pantomimists and knockabout tumblers, presenting an act that combined acrobatics, stilt walking and eccentric dancing. Archie had doubtless met them during their 1917 engagement in Bristol, and he quite possibly heard how difficult it was for Pender to keep his teenaged performers when they reached the age of 18, as they were swiftly swallowed up by the Army and sent to fight in Europe, leaving the troupe almost perpetually in need of new members.

Joining up with Pender would require some subterfuge. Having only just turned 14 ... although he was tall for his age ... Archie didn't meet the minimum age requirement. However, this did not deter him, and he wrote a letter to Bob Pender, pretending to be his father and signing Elias's name, lying about his age. He included a recent photograph which Archie felt made him look more mature, and he sent the letter off. He dutifully kept an eye out for each day's postal deliveries, until he finally found a return letter from Pender. Slipping away with it before his father saw it, he opened it up and was amazed to not only find that Pender was extending an invitation for Archie to join him but had even included rail fare for the young man to make the trip to Norwich, where the troupe was then performing.

Archie packed a few belongings into a bag, and without telling his family anything, he simply walked out of the house one morning, and boarded the train. The journey, which included changing trains in London, took a good part of the day, and when he arrived in Norwich, he wasted no time in seeking out Pender at the theatre where the troupe was performing.

Putting the teenager through his paces, Pender quickly realized that Archie had little experience at tumbling, but he had a natural athletic ability, and was unafraid to try something, even at the risk of failing, which was a key asset in their line of work. With enough training, Pender was confident that young Mr. Leach would fit in with the team.

Any newcomer goes through a degree of hazing from his fellows, and it was no different for Archie. Though, his charm and disposition quickly won him friends within the troupe, and he was speedily accepted into the ranks. He was picking up their basic routines in short order, and even proving adept at stilt walking. It was all that the young teen could have hoped for.

Then it all very nearly came to a crashing end.

Archie's scheme to wrangle an invite to the troupe had worked a bit too well. Pender had not caught on to the fact that it had been the cunning teenager he had initially dealt with by mail, and so he thought nothing of posting a progress report on the boy to Elias Leach. At last, discovering the whereabouts of his runaway son, Elias arrived several days later to collect the wayward lad, who was distraught at the idea of going back home to Bristol.

When Pender told him how well Archie was getting on with the troupe, and how skillful he was starting to become at tumbling, the elder Leach began to reconsider bringing the boy home. Perhaps he contemplated that, having been ejected from school, there was really nothing waiting for Archie in Bristol other than the search for a job . . . and having him with the Penders did mean one less mouth to feed for Elias.

After further discussion, Leach agreed to let Archie remain with the troupe, provided he be signed to a proper contract that guaranteed him a weekly wage, thus offering him a degree of employment security. That accomplished, Elias returned home to Bristol alone, and Archie was now fully on his own.

In the weeks and months that followed, Archie reveled at being a part of the troupe. It was more than a mere job . . . it was in many ways the family life he had never known before. Bob and Maggie Pender ran the group with discipline, insisting that the performers adhere to strict training schedules and that they observe exact times to go to bed, to wake up, and to have breakfast, but they were not martinets. They treated the members of the troupe almost as extensions of their own family. The underage members actually lived with the Penders in their own London home, and inevitably Bob and Margaret became surrogate parents to Archie.

He responded well to the Penders' discipline, and they in turn grew very fond of the wiry boy, appreciating his polite manners and his willingness to work hard to learn the tumbling trade. Archie also realized a sense of wanderlust as the troupe traveled throughout Britain, allowing him to discover the wonders of various cities, in particular London, which he loved to tour aboard an open top double decker bus, taking in the imperial sights of the capital.

With the end of the war in November of 1918, many former members of the troupe returned from their military services, allowing Pender to create two touring troupes to work simultaneously. Archie was irked that he was assigned to what he considered to be the lesser troupe, which usually toured smaller cities in often less-than-splendid theatrical settings, but he worked hard to shine among his fellow performers, in the hopes of being elevated to the main group.

He'd get that chance in the summer of 1920, when Bob Pender announced that he had signed to have a group of eight performers work on Broadway in New York City. It was only a two-week booking, but Pender was confident that once they were there, he could get them further work in vaudeville houses. To Archie's great relief and excitement, he was selected to be a part of the America-bound group.

On July 20th, Archie and the rest of the troupe boarded the RMS Olympic, the sister ship of the ill-fated Titanic, and set sail for America. Also aboard were two of the most famous people in the

Western world, film stars Douglas Fairbanks and Mary Pickford, who were returning from their European honeymoon. Pickford tended to spend much of the trip in her quarters, already having been exhausted by the throngs of fans who mobbed them on the Continent, and now wished nothing but peace and quiet on the voyage home. But Fairbanks liked to do his morning calisthenics on the deck, where he happily signed autographs and mingled with the other passengers. Archie was thrilled to meet him, and the actor ...with his powerful physique, dazzling smile, golden bronzed tan and robustly jaunty demeanor ... made a deep and lasting impression on the 16-year-old. In years to come, Cary Grant would do more than a little to emulate the look and behavior of Doug Fairbanks.

After a week on the Atlantic, the ship was nearing shore. Too excited to sleep, Archie stayed up all night, and stood at the railing as America loomed into view in the early dawn hour. The Statue of Liberty and the skyscrapers, all taller than any building in England, filled his eyes and fired his imagination.

After disembarking and going through customs, the troupe was collected by a representative of Charles Dillingham, who was producing the show they were scheduled for, and they were taken to the Globe Theater. It was there that Bob Pender made a disappointing discovery, as he could tell at-a-glance that the Globe's stage was too shallow for many of the troupe's routines, and the ceiling too low for their stilt-walking act, and just like that, the visiting Brits were struck from the performance line-up. Mercifully however, Pender was told that Dillingham was also at that time producing a large-scale spectacle show at the Hippodrome, and most likely he could find a place for the troupe in that production.

The New York Hippodrome billed itself as the largest theater in the world, with a 100x200 foot stage and seating capacity for some 5,300. Dillingham's production, *Good Times* (1920), featuring a variety of acts, from comedic bicyclist Joe Jackson and singer Belle Story, to the Hanneford Family trick horsemen and the world-famous clown, Marceline, not to mention diving girls, elephants ... and after a quick negotiation, the Pender troupe.

They were initially booked for only a two-week run, but they proved to be an instant hit with audiences, and so not only was their on-stage time increased, but their run was extended for nearly an entire year, until the end of season.

If it was hardly fame and fortune for young Archie . . . he was only an anonymous minor performer earning a modest weekly sum, after all . . . the excitement of being on Broadway more than made up for it.

After *Good Times*, Pender got the troupe bookings on vaudeville circuits across the United States and into Canada, but upon turning 18, Archie announced he was leaving the company and returning home to England. Pender was sorry to see him go, and tried to talk him into staying, but the young man was adamant that he had made up his mind. Pender graciously bought him a ticket back home . . . but soon enough was surprised and disappointed to learn that Archie in fact did not go back to England, but instead had cashed in his ticket and was using that money to support himself while he sought work as an actor in New York City. Archie's deception drove a wedge between him and Bob Pender, and they never again enjoyed the surrogate familial relationship they had known.

Thus began nearly a decade in which Archie Leach struggled to establish himself as a stage actor. It was slow going, and difficult at times. It got off to an inauspicious start, when the only work he could find was as a stilt-walker at Coney Island. At one point he was reduced to hawking ties on street corners, hand made by one of his roommates, a fellow struggling actor named Jack Kelly (who, as Orry-Kelly, later went on to be an Academy Award-winning costume designer for such films as *An American in Paris* (1951) and *Some Like It Hot* {1959}). When he did land theatrical work, it was often only in bit parts. It had to have been discouraging.

Archie never gave up. Instead, he slowly learned his craft. In truth, he wasn't a natural actor, and it was a good long while before he could deliver a line without sounding stilted or self-conscious. In time he began to learn the skills needed to convincingly play a role in front of an audience. He would avidly watch fellow actors and pick up whatever tricks of the trade they could impart.

Just as importantly, he also created *himself.* By the end of the Twenties, as Archie Leach was at last starting to earn some positive attention on the stage, he was about as far away from the kid who arrived as a part of Pender's troupe, as Bristol was from New York. The earnestness, the amiability, and above all the charm were still there in abundance. However, he had developed a physical gracefulness that drew eyes upon him. Quite frankly, he landed more than a few roles mostly because he looked so good moving across the stage, rather than for his dramatic talents.

What also made him distinctive was his voice. It was quite unlike anyone else's...and quite distinct from the West Country Bristolian of his youth (flecked with the bits of Cockney he picked up during his time with the Penders in London). Whether consciously or not ...and most likely this was fully intentional...Archie sculpted an amalgam of his native British tongue with what is known as the Mid-Atlantic accent, which was developed along the Eastern Seaboard of the United States and adopted primarily by the well-to-do. Its English antecedents are immediately obvious, but no Brit would confuse it for any inflection from the U.K. In the early 20th Century, Mid-Atlantic was very much in vogue among actors, and therefore Archie would have heard it spoken daily. Always anxious to fit in during those years, it's no surprise that Archie adopted the accent for himself, but coming from an already established British pronunciation, it metamorphosed into something quite unique, and decidedly memorable (for examples of Mid-Atlantic as spoken by American-born actors, one need only listen to Katharine Hepburn, born in Hartford, Connecticut, Irene Dunne, from Louisville, Kentucky, and Vincent Price, of St. Louis, Missouri.)

He finally began to enjoy true success in 1927. Following a successful six month run in *Golden Dawn* (1927), Archie was signed by producer Arthur Hammerstein to a long-term contract. Just a few months after that, producer Florenz Ziegfeld inquired about picking up Archie's contract. But Hammerstein and Ziegfeld were long-time rivals, and Hammerstein refused the request largely out of spite. However, as Archie had openly expressed enthusiasm for working for Ziegfeld, his loyalty to Hammerstein was now called into question, putting his future with the producer in jeopardy. It was then that, yet another Broadway dynasty entered the picture, as J.J. and Lee Shubert bought out Archie's contract from Hammerstein.

They offered him a two-year deal at a very respectable $350 a week, but to their surprise, Archie declined the offer, and instead insisted on a non-exclusive pact with run-of-the-show guarantees. That way, if other acting opportunities arose in-between Shubert plays, he was free to pursue them. Archie simply wasn't comfortable leaving his fate in the hands of others, and wanted to be able to seize any brass rings that happened to pass within his grasp.

His first production with them was a musical called *Boom Boom* (1929), in which he co-starred with Jeanette MacDonald. The critics savaged the play, and it managed to limp along for only 72 performances, but it did lead to one new possibility which intrigued the rising young actor.

Sound had arrived in motion pictures, and in 1929 Metro-Goldwyn-Mayer released *Broadway Melody* (1929), the first 'all-talkie' film musical, a bona fide box office smash. Suddenly, all the movie studios were scrambling to make their own musicals, and they were rushing to Broadway to find the singing actors to fill them. Archie and Jeanette were both invited to make a screen test for Paramount at their Astoria studio in Queens, New York.

The test is now lost to history, but its results are known to us. For MacDonald, it meant an offer to come to Hollywood, where she launched a long and highly successful film career. Archie received only an embarrassing rejection, as Paramount turned him down. It may not have been his acting abilities which did him in, so much as his physical appearance; the casting director told him there would be no place for him in pictures because, "You're bow-legged and your neck is too thick."

Hollywood's loss remained the Shuberts' gain, as they continued casting Archie, first on Broadway in *A Wonderful Night* (1929), then in the touring company of *The Street Singer* (1929). By summer of 1931, the Shuberts had assigned him to a summer stock company in St. Louis in the period between the Broadway seasons (few New York City theaters ran productions in the stifling summertime because almost none of them had air conditioning.)

At that moment in time, all was well for the actor. He was working steadily, earning excellent money, getting good notices from the newspapers, and proving to be a very popular guest at fashionable dinner parties. However, Archie could read the writing on the wall ... and count the increasingly empty seats in the theaters. As the Great Depression grew worse, fewer and fewer people had the discretionary income to see live plays, and he was hearing the backstage rumors about the Shuberts being in worsening financial straits ... a rumor proven true when they suddenly informed the cast that they would all have to take a substantial cut in salary. Archie knew full well what the probable outcome would be: his contract would soon be terminated in a cost-cutting move, and he might very well find himself stranded in the Midwest.

Weighing his options, Archie boldly struck first, insisting that the Shuberts either continue to guarantee his original salary, or they should release him from his contract. Teetering on the verge of bankruptcy, the Shuberts opted for the latter, and Archie Leach was once again a free agent on Broadway.

Luckily, he didn't have to pound the pavement for very long looking for his next part. At that moment, actress Fay Wray was preparing to star in *Nikki* (1931), written by her husband, John Monk Saunders. The play's producer had read a complimentary notice about Archie's work in St. Louis and asked him to come read for the role of Cary Lockwood, Wray's romantic lead. He did, and not only impressed the producer, director, and playwright, but also developed a fast rapport with Fay Wray.

Simultaneous with this, another unexpected development emerged. Casey Robinson, a producer at Paramount's Astoria Studio, needed to cast four singing sailors in a one-reel short film, *Singapore Sue* (1932), starring Chinese actress Anna Chang. Searching through screen tests, he happened upon the one which Archie had made with Jeanette MacDonald two years previous, and thick neck and bowlegs aside, he liked what he saw in the actor. Would Archie be interested in making the film?

He was indeed. It would only take a few days and would provide him with some extra cash ... and who knew, maybe it would lead at long last to a Hollywood contract of his own.

It didn't. In fact, *Singapore Sue* (1932) wasn't even released until more than a year later to a middling response, at which point fate had already intervened in the life of Archie Leach.

Meanwhile, despite high hopes, *Nikki* (1931) closed in just a month. With more theaters going dark as the economy worsened, the prospect of finding another production anytime soon seemed slim, so Archie decided to make use of his *Singapore Sue* (1932) money, and accompanied by a friend, composer Phil Charig, he planned to drive his Packard Phaeton convertible South to Florida, where the two of them would spend a few weeks golfing, but just prior to their departure, Archie received a phone call from Fay Wray. Immediately after the end of *Nikki* (1931), she and her husband had headed to Hollywood, where she had been acting in films since the silent era, and he became an Academy Award winning screenwriter. Wray and Saunders had become good friends with Archie, and she now suggested he spend his vacation in California visiting them. Archie and Charig headed West.

There was by this point a steady exodus of Broadway talent to Hollywood, but to everyone in New York, Archie insisted this was strictly a pleasure trip, and pointed out that he had even agreed to appear in a new Shubert production shortly after his return to the East Coast in January. Later he admitted that privately he had decided the time had come to throw his lot in with the movies, and he was determined to get one of the big studios to sign him.

Archie and Phil arrived in Los Angeles just after Thanksgiving of 1931. One thing the actor had long since learned was that appearances matter when it comes to the entertainment business, and you're more likely to find success if you carry yourself as if you are already successful. As a result, there would be no budget rooming houses during his stay in LA . . . he checked into the luxurious Château Élysée, home to such film stars as Edward G. Robinson and Lillian Gish. Reaching out to various Broadway friends who had already established themselves in California, Archie quickly found himself on the guest lists of dinner parties, greeted at top speakeasies, and even welcomed as a popular weekend newcomer at publishing tycoon William Randolph Hearst's fabled San Simeon estate. The result was that he was making himself known in Hollywood circles and putting his charm to its best possible use.

A friend of Archie's back in New York City, William Morris talent agent Billy Grady, promised the actor an introduction to prominent Hollywood agent Walter Herzbrun, who took an immediate liking to the handsome and robust young man. Herzbrun thought that a friend of his who was also a relative newcomer to Hollywood, Marion Gering, might offer some good advice to the actor on navigating the studio system, so he invited both men to lunch in order to meet one another. It's possible that Archie already knew of Gering -- who was born in Russia and had come to the United States in 1924 as a member of the Soviet Trade Commission, but promptly defected and pursued his dream of being a playwright and stage director – as he had enjoyed several successes on Broadway before coming to California to direct films.

Like Herzbrun, Gering was likewise impressed by Archie, and within a few days of their lunch, invited the actor to join him for dinner with B.P. Schulberg, the production chief of Paramount Studios. Gering was careful to not overtly pitch Archie to the studio boss, knowing that Schulberg would be resistant to such a blatant sell. Instead, the conversation meandered over a variety of subjects, including Archie's stage work as well as his brief foray (and as of yet still unreleased) into filmmaking with *Singapore Sue* (1932), when finally, the director casually mentioned that he would be shooting a screen test for his wife, actress Dorothy Libaire, the following day. Schulberg, who knew exactly what Gering was subtly hinting at, just as casually said that Archie might like to drop by the studio and read lines on camera to Libaire.

The next day, Archie Leach stepped onto the soundstage at the Paramount Famous Players Lasky Studio, looking relaxed and cheerful. With the camera rolling, he delivered his lines with an ease that far surpassed his rather stilted, stagey performance in *Singapore Sue* (1932). Later, reviewing the screen test, B.P. Schulberg and his executives came to two conclusions: first, that Dorothy Libaire was not worth pursuing for the studio, and secondly, that Archie Leach most definitely was.

A few days later, Archie was again a guest at San Simeon when a call arrived for him. Ordinarily, Hearst didn't like for film business to intrude upon his idylls, but Schulberg was too important a figure to be denied, and he was calling personally for Mr. Leach. Picking up the receiver, Archie heard the news he was waiting for: Paramount was offering him a five-year contract (with options to continue or cancel, at the studio's discretion, every six months), with a beginning salary of $450 a week, and the promise of regular raises. "One other thing," Schulberg added almost as an afterthought, "If you accept, you'll have to change your name."

Accepting was an easy decision. The hard one was deciding what he would now call himself. Fay Wray suggested that he adopt the name of his character from *Nikki* (1931), Cary Lockwood. Archie liked it, and took it to Schulberg, who thought that Cary was fine, but he nixed Lockwood, arguing that at eight letters in length, it would look crowded on a theater marquee. Pick something shorter, he was told...and make it memorable.

As the actor later recounted, "A secretary brought me a list and I simply closed my eyes and stuck a pin into it and came up with 'Grant'." By all accounts, it really wasn't much more complex than that. Schulberg approved, in part because it gave his newest contractee the same initials...albeit in reverse order...as Paramount's biggest star, Gary Cooper. It seemed like a good omen.

Just like that, Archie Leach ceased to exist. Cary Grant would consign those 28 years of life . . . Bristol, his parents, the Pender troupe, Broadway...into the receding past, and create a daring new future for himself. He made this passage without hesitation, and the only seeming sentimentality for the boy and man he was, he displayed when he later got himself a dog and named him "Archie Leach".

The studio wasted no time putting their newest employee to work. Unlike most Hollywood newcomers, who generally started out in small, often non-speaking parts, and worked their way up to larger roles, Grant was given a major part in his very first film, *This Is the Night* (1932), being fifth billed behind such established performers as Lili Damita, Charles Ruggles, Roland Young and Thelma Todd. Rapidly shot and released in just a little over three months after Grant's signing, it did fair at the box office, and he received some good notices in his debut. However, seeing himself on the big screen for the first time, Grant was mortified by what he deemed to be an awful performance, and he decided then and there to quit films and go back to the theater. Fortunately, he was talked out of this by friends, who explained to him that his reaction was not uncommon for film newcomers, and at any rate, one simply doesn't walk out of a major studio contract. Reassured, he dutifully reported back to Paramount for his next feature film.

=2=
1932 - 1936

The Great Depression years had been particularly rough for Paramount Pictures. An over-expansion of their already vast theater holdings, along with the rapid conversion to sound in each of those theaters, had driven the company to take on ever-mounting debt. Since 1930, the studio's ledger had ended each year awash in red ink. In this they were not alone; of all of Hollywood's major studios during the first half of the Thirties…Paramount, Metro-Goldwyn-Mayer (MGM), Warner Bros., RKO, Fox, Universal…only MGM had managed to consistently turn a profit. Paramount had gone into receivership in 1933, and in 1935 the company finally bowed to the unavoidable and filed for bankruptcy in order to reorganize.

But through it all, Paramount never slowed its pace in the production of films. Each year the studio averaged sixty or more features, plus shorts, newsreels, and animated cartoons. The chain of Paramount-owned theaters insatiably needed new product week after week, thus guaranteeing screens available for Paramount movies in many American cities. And where there were no Paramount theaters, independent theater owners were subject to block booking, the process by which a theater would be guaranteed, for instance, the next Gary Cooper film (almost certain to be a box office success), but only in exchange for agreeing to also show multiple other lesser Paramount films during the year[1].

The result was, with such an unrelenting demand for films, Cary Grant found himself working constantly. In 1932 alone he had significant roles in no fewer than seven feature films. As he steadily worked his way up to leading man, he co-starred in several major productions for Paramount … *Blonde Venus* (1932) with Marlene Dietrich, *The Eagle and the Hawk* (1933) with Fredric March and

---

1 The U.S. Supreme Court declared block booking to be an illegal trade practice in *United States v. Paramount Pictures, Inc. et al*, 1948.

Carole Lombard, and a pair of films that were as popular as they were controversial, *She Done Him Wrong* (1933) and *I'm No Angel* (1933), both starring Mae West.

After those early successes, Grant's career seemed to plateau. He was still a leading man, but over the next few years he saw himself cast in films that fell short of Paramount's 'A List'. Not that motion pictures such as *Kiss and Make-Up* (1934), *Ladies Should Listen* (1934) and *Enter Madame* (1935) were not entertaining, but they were not made nor marketed on a par with such major productions as *Cleopatra* (1934) and *The Lives of a Bengal Lancer* (1935), both of which were nominees for the Best Picture Academy Awards in their respective years.

Even more frustrating for Grant was that he felt himself being typecast as what was dismissively considered a "mannequin"; that is, as a handsome man known best for looking good in a suit or tuxedo, rather than for his acting skills. Not that he considered himself to be all that great of an actor...yet...but he knew he was made for better things than just the sharpness of his jawline or how well he could casually sit without spoiling the crease of his pants. Maddeningly, Paramount no longer seemed all that interested in giving him opportunities to prove himself.

Ironically, but not all that unexpectedly, when such a chance did arise, it wasn't with Paramount at all. With no new film available for him at that moment, the studio loaned[2] him to RKO, where he co-starred with Katharine Hepburn in *Sylvia Scarlett* (1935). Upon its release, the film was seen by many as a misstep bordering on all-out disaster. On seeing the final cut, both Hepburn and director George Cukor begged RKO to never release it, and most critics shared their opinion. Audiences stayed away in droves, and the film lost over $350,000.

But one person came away from *Sylvia Scarlett* (1935) considering it something of a triumph: Cary Grant. Given a role with actual depth, playing opposite such an accomplished actress as Hepburn, and in the hands of so sympathetic a director as Cukor, Grant truly

---

2 "Loaning" was a system by which studios would allow their contract actors to work for another studio, either in exchange for an actor (or director) from the other studio, or cash, or both. Loans were approved or rejected solely by studio heads, and the actors themselves had little or no say over the practice.

blossomed. He was able to shed the 'man about town' persona that he was made to inhabit repeatedly at Paramount, and stretch his abilities in the role of Jimmy Monkley, including employing the Cockney accent he had picked up in his Pender days. As much as the critics didn't like the film, many of them made a point of singling Grant out for praise, giving him some of his best reviews yet.

Time would eventually bring about a sea change in the critical appraisals of the film, and a few decades later it was reassessed as a great motion picture that was simply too far ahead of its time to find an audience in 1935. While *Scarlett* did little to enhance Grant's drawing power at the box office, it bolstered his confidence and made him more determined than ever to improve the quality of his roles. However, Paramount saw no reason not to continue things exactly as they were. After all, the films that Grant had been doing for them were usually more modestly budgeted, and almost always returned a good profit, which was of acute importance as the studio struggled out of the mire of bankruptcy. Why risk that, they thought?

If Grant had returned from his sojourn to RKO hoping that Paramount might now cast him opposite their biggest female star, Claudette Colbert, or be placed in the hands of one of the studio's leading directors, such as Ernst Lubitsch or Henry Hathaway, he was soon left sorely disappointed, as he read through the script of his next assignment, *Big Brown Eyes* (1936). Certainly not a bad story, but nevertheless not much different from most everything else he had already made over the past two years. It would be helmed by journeyman director Raoul Walsh . . . still several years away from creating such classic hits as *The Roaring Twenties* (1939) and *High Sierra* (1941) . . . and Cary would be playing opposite Joan Bennett, whose recent career like Grant's had been consigned to secondary assignments.

More infuriating still was that MGM had specifically requested Grant to play the third lead in their biggest production of 1935, *Mutiny on the Bounty*, co-starring Clark Gable and Charles Laughton. However, for reasons unexplained to Grant (but probably stemming from one of the frequent spats that erupted between rival studio heads), Paramount flatly refused to loan him out. He had to watch from afar as *Mutiny* went on to become one of MGM's biggest box office and critical hits of the year ... as well as see Franchot Tone, who was cast for the role of "Byam" that was originally meant for Grant, be nominated for an Academy Award. Adding insult to injury, several months later Paramount did loan Grant to MGM for *Suzy* (1936), an overwrought and relatively slight romantic drama starring Jean Harlow, with Grant third-billed ... behind Franchot Tone.

He was entering the final year of his five-year contract. While his Hollywood career could by no stretch of the imagination be considered unsuccessful (he was making some $2,500 a week, after all), in Grant's estimation, he was not where he should be in the pantheon of stars. Additionally, he was not holding out hope for Paramount to make any serious effort to improve his situation. The studio's biggest star remained Gary Cooper, who continued to have first pick of film roles. More ominous still from Grant's viewpoint, Paramount had a new leading man, Fred MacMurray, and they were grooming him with the kinds of roles that Cary wanted: *The Gilded Lily* (1935), co-starring Claudette Colbert and directed by Wesley Ruggles, and *Hands Across the Table* (1935), opposite Carole Lombard, with direction by Mitchell Leisen. Worse still from Grant's viewpoint, MacMurray had also been loaned to RKO in '35 to co-star with Katherine Hepburn for director George Stevens. Their film, *Alice Adams* (1935), had been both a critical and box office hit, and was nominated for the Best Film Academy Award.

Despite its relatively brief history as an industry, Hollywood was nonetheless littered with the faded recollections of actors who had risen to stardom, only to see themselves plummet from the heights into obscurity. Cary didn't have to look far for examples. Men like Richard Arlen, Chester Morris and Neil Hamilton had all been top billed names when Grant had arrived in Hollywood, but by the mid-Thirties each had seen their careers slipping from major productions to 'B' fare ... often with their billing descending as well. That these actors had been bumped from prominence by the likes of Cary Grant was an irony not lost on the Englishman. "Becoming a movie star is something like getting on a streetcar. Actors and actresses are packed in like sardines." Cary opined years later. "A few stood, holding tightly to leather straps to avoid being pushed aside. Others were firmly seated in the center of the car. They were the big stars. At the front, new actors and actresses pushed and shoved to get aboard. Some made it and slowly moved toward the center. When a new 'star' came aboard, an old one had to be edged out the rear exit. The crowd was so big you were pushed right off. There was room for only so many and no more."

In 1936, Cary Grant felt he was standing in the back half of the streetcar, holding a strap. He wanted to sit down, but he had increasing doubts that Paramount was going to do much to help him find a seat.

•••

As tumultuous as his career seemed to him, his personal life had been even more turbulent during these years, as if the cost for his public success was private turmoil. His life was turned upside down when he discovered that his mother was in fact not deceased as his father had told him, but instead had been institutionalized in a sanitarium for many years.

As with so many other events in the life of Cary Grant, the details conflict with one another, in no small part because Grant himself would give contradictory versions over the years, never entirely comfortable with fully revealing himself to anyone. Most likely it was in late 1933[3], when he made his first visit back to Britain since he set sail for America thirteen years before, that he learned the truth. He came up from London to Bristol to finally see his father and family. As Grant had told it, he and Elias reconciled with one another and had a grand time, but as other family members later stated, there was a marked coolness between father and son. All accounts agree that Elias Leach was in wretched physical shape, the result of decades of alcoholism and resultant illnesses, and that when Grant first laid eyes on him, he could scarcely believe this was the same man he had known growing up.

Taking his son to a local pub for pints, Elias informed Cary that Elsie was still alive. In some tellings, the elder Leach was deeply

---

3 Some accounts place it in 1935.

remorseful, insisting that he had only lied to Archie for all those years to spare him the burden of knowing that his mother was mentally ill. In some less charitable reports, Elias took a perverse joy in 'taking the piss' out of his movie star son and expressed no real regret over having hidden the truth.

Either way, the news hit Grant like a wrecking ball.

Again, accounts differ as to what happened next. Either Grant hastened to Fishponds, the hospital where Elsie was living, to see her face to face for the first time in nearly two decades, or else their reunion came two years later, on a subsequent visit by Grant to England to shoot a film. And when they did see each other again, either it was a loving reunion, or Elsie denied that this "Cary Grant" fellow could possibly be her little boy, Archie. Or else, she did accept it, but still displayed virtually no maternal affection for her son. One thing that is for sure, great stock can be placed in Grant's later revelation that he dealt with receiving the bombshell news of his mother's existence by going on a grand drunken dayslong bender.

Whatever the case may be, it could not have produced anything other than emotional uproar for Cary. He responded to it in an equally disorienting manner: he got married.

His romantic relationship with actress Virginia Cherrill was intense and passionate, but also fraught with arguments, breakups, and reconciliations, and although they had spoken of marriage, few of those who knew them believed Grant would ever consent. However, with the new-found knowledge about his mother's existence, Grant decided that marriage would provide him with much-needed stability. In this, he was quickly and sadly proven wrong. The attraction between Grant and Cherrill, both two stunningly beautiful specimens, was largely physical. But outside of sex, they seemed to have little in common. It also didn't help that their careers were going in opposite trajectories.

Like Grant, Cherrill achieved film success very nearly from the start, when Charlie Chaplin plucked her from obscurity to co-star in his 1931 film, *City Lights*. But Cherrill was not a trained actress, and while Chaplin was able to coax a sensitive performance out of her, other directors (including John Ford) could not in her subsequent films. Her career quickly slid down from the heights, and by the time she and Grant were wed she was seventh-billed in a Charlie Chan programmer for Fox.

Their marriage became an ongoing string of angry quarrels and sulking separations. According to Cherrill, Grant became blindly jealous of any man who so much as smiled at her, and he became convinced she was having affairs behind his back. He ended many nights drunk and verbally abusive, she claimed.

Married on February 9th of 1934, they were legally divorced by March 26th, 1935, with Cherrill accusing Grant of having subjected her to mental and physical cruelty. Grant disputed the charges that he had ever struck her, but he did admit that they had developed irreconcilable differences. As he later reflected, "My possessiveness and fear of losing Virginia brought about the very condition I feared: the loss of her." By 1936 Cherrill's dwindling film career wound down to a close, and the year after she married George Child-Villiers, the 9th Earl of Jersey, moving to England to be the Countess of Jersey.

Single once more, Cary found no shortage of gorgeous ladies anxious to occupy his time. He dated actresses Mary Brian, Betty Furness and Elissa Landi, and socialite Bobby Cooper, but soon became serious with one specific woman. Phyllis Brooks was a 20-year-old model who had come to Hollywood, and had landed a number of bit parts in films, usually uncredited, the most noteworthy being 1934's *The Man Who Reclaimed His Head*, which despite its title (and the fact that it was produced by Universal, the home of *Dracula* {1931} and *Frankenstein* {1931}), was not a horror picture, but rather a Claude Raines-led drama. Whereas her film career wasn't setting the silver screen ablaze, Brooks . . . vivacious, funny, clever, and very beautiful . . . instantly became a popular guest on the Hollywood social circuit, being invited to the best parties. In fact, she and Grant had crossed paths on the party scene frequently, until finally Grant asked her out for an evening of dancing. From there, they became an item, as he was near besotted by the diverting incongruity of her risqué humor and graceful charms. Hollywood columnists breathlessly followed their public dates, and soon enough were predicting wedding bells.

Increasingly smitten with Brooks, Grant went so far as suggesting marriage to her (he had also asked Mary Brian to marry him shortly after his divorce from Cherrill, but then very quickly backed away from that, and soon thereafter ended the relationship with her altogether.) But he was also reluctant to agree to just when they should be wed. Brooks, who seemed to understand Grant's commitment issues and was patient enough to try and ride them out, made it plain she was ready to marry him whenever he was willing…but that he shouldn't wait *too* long. Still, he would not make a definite decision.

●●●

While all these romantic developments took place, Grant also entered into another relationship, one which had even more far-reaching and long-lasting…indeed, life changing…consequences for the actor.

Frank W. Vincent and Archie Leach first met back in New York when Vincent booked some dates for the Pender Troupe on the Orpheum theater vaudeville circuit, and they apparently interacted enough to make favorable impressions on one another. Several years later, as Archie was making his way as a struggling actor on Broadway, they renewed their acquaintanceship and it developed into a genuine friendship. In 1932 Vincent left New York City and the theatrical world behind and came to Los Angeles, where he became an agent in partnership with Harry E. Edington. Their agency eventually became a powerhouse in Hollywood as the pair came to represent Greta Garbo, Marlene Dietrich, Douglas Fairbanks, Jr., Edward G. Robinson, and Joel McCrea, among others. Also on their roster was Cary Grant, but what was known only to a few was that Grant was more than just another actor they represented…he was a silent partner in the agency itself.

When Grant first arrived in Hollywood, he decided it would be a smart idea to augment his studio salary with a business investment, particularly knowing that Paramount could release him at their discretion after each six-month interval. After becoming acquainted with a decorator named Robert Lampe, and a salesman named L. Wright Neale, the trio decided to pool their resources and establish an upscale men's clothing store on Wilshire Blvd. in May of 1932. They called it Neale's, as it would be publicly fronted by its namesake, who would oversee all business matters. But soon enough, troubling warning signs began to appear as past due notices for everything from the rent to the electric bill found their way to Grant. Just two months after the venture was launched, L. Wright Neale absconded with as much of the store's capital he could pocket, and Grant was left responsible for debts that were more than double his initial investment in the business.

His fingers badly singed by that debacle, but still wanting to establish a supplemental income to his Paramount earnings, Grant decided that throwing in with his friend Vincent, along with Edington, who had a reputation for integrity in Hollywood, was a much safer bet, and he invested in their agency. It would prove to be a much more lucrative gamble than a haberdashery.

With the five-year contract he signed in December of 1931 in its final few months, Paramount duly informed Grant that they would like to renew his deal. He turned the negotiations over to Vincent, but with some very explicit instructions. First of all, he wanted money that reflected his status ... or what he felt his status should be ... in the Hollywood firmament. Vincent didn't think that would be all that difficult to get, as Paramount undoubtedly knew it was in their better interest to not lose the popular star that they had built up from scratch. Gary Cooper's own contract was set to expire later in 1937, and it was an open secret on the lot that studio executives were prepared to offer him one of filmdom's biggest salaries in order to keep him[4]. It was the least Paramount could do, Grant reasoned, to show some financial generosity to him as well.

A more difficult sell would be Grant's insistence that he have contractual guarantees giving him a say in what films he made, as well as input into who his directors and leading ladies would be. While Paramount might be willing to give Cooper or Mae West

---

4 Nevertheless, although Paramount would eventually offer Cooper an extravagant $8,000 a week, he shocked the executives by rejecting the contract, leaving the studio, and signing on with independent producer Samuel Goldwyn instead.

an unofficial voice in the discussions over which movies they made (and that was a rare high privilege in Hollywood -- neither MGM extended the same courtesy to Clark Gable, nor Warner Bros. to James Cagney, for instance), they were by no means willing to codify that in ink for anyone. If this privilege were to be sanctioned for Grant, then not only Cooper and West, but all the studio's other top rank stars . . . Claudette Colbert, Marlene Dietrich, Bing Crosby, Carole Lombard, George Raft . . . would demand the same as well. It would utterly undermine the power of the studio to control their talent and shape their careers as Paramount's executives desired . . . and the contagion would doubtless spread to other studios as well. The agent explained this to his client, but the actor told him he didn't care. If Paramount wouldn't agree to these terms, Grant said, find another studio that would.

Although Paramount offered Grant a boost in pay to an impressive $3,500 a week, they refused to budge on his other demands. He rejected the offer and told his agent to start speaking with other studios, but Frank Vincent had a different idea. He knew the odds of any major studio in Hollywood agreeing to Grant's terms were slim to none, and while one of the smaller "Poverty Row" producers, such as Republic or Monogram, might be willing to provide the actor with such guarantees in exchange for adding a marquee name to their roster, they couldn't possibly deliver a salary comparable to what Paramount was offering, nor offer the kind of quality productions that Grant was anxious to make. However, the venturous-thinking agent had a theory that at least some of the "major minors" . . . Columbia, Universal, United Artists . . . might just be interested in agreeing to Grant's demands, if only in return for short, non-exclusive deals.

The result would be for Cary Grant to voluntarily exit the Hollywood studio system, the all-prevailing structure that was at the very foundation of the industry, and to have him strike out on his own, as a freelancer. To anyone with a lick of sense in the movie capital, it seemed like a sure path to career suicide, but Frank Vincent believed, despite all the risks, that such a path could instead lead to tremendous success for the right actor, and he felt with remarkable certainty that his client was *that* actor.

Once the audacious idea was outlined, Grant took some time to ponder it. He spoke with friends, some of whom were intrigued by the notion, and others who said he'd be a fool to sacrifice a sure thing by not staying with Paramount. Finally, he made up his mind and told Vincent to get to work.

Cary Grant was declaring his independence.

1937

It was fitting that when Grant's Paramount contract finally expired, he was working, but not at Paramount. Instead, the studio had loaned him to RKO for *Robber Barons* (although it would soon be retitled *The Toast of New York* upon its release in early 1937*)*, a loosely factual biopic of scandalous 19th Century financier James Fisk, with the leading role filled by Edward Arnold. Arnold was one of those rare Hollywood stories of a successful character actor finding himself elevated to top billing . . . although nearing fifty and heavyset (otherwise complimentary film fan magazines at the time cheerily described him as "beefy" and "fairly fat"), he was far from anyone's ideal of a silver screen leading man. Which was why producer Edward Small cast Grant in the film, so that Grant could provide the sex appeal.

The production became a desultory ordeal, with constant script revisions. Yet the story was never more than boilerplate romantic melodrama, with a love triangle between business partners Fisk and Nick Boyd (Grant's character,) and Josie Mansfield, played by Frances Farmer. A mid-production change in directors added to the muddle, and the shooting dragged on from the scheduled eight weeks to fifteen. Worse still for Grant was the fact that he couldn't develop a personal rapport with his leading lady, Farmer, and they maintained an aloof distance when they weren't romancing one another in front of the camera.

Amid filming *The Toast of New York* (1937), Grant had one last bit of Paramount business to attend to. Although he had left the company's employ just days before, in early January Grant returned to the studio as one of nearly 500 invited guests who fêted Paramount Pictures co-founder and chairman of the board Adolph Zukor on his silver jubilee in the filmmaking industry. While Grant was disappointed that the studio had not agreed with his contract demands, necessitating his departure, he harbored no grudge, and he was genuinely appreciative of Zukor, B.P. Schulberg, and other studio executives who had launched his Hollywood career. Grant had a grand time that evening, in what would prove to be his last visit to a Paramount soundstage until he made Alfred Hitchcock's *To Catch a Thief* in 1955.

As filming of *The Toast of New York* dragged on, Frank Vincent opened negotiations with Columbia Pictures first and then shortly thereafter RKO Radio Pictures. It was a fortuitous time to offer the services of a leading man of Cary Grant's stature to both studios, as each was in need of just that sort of marquee asset. At that point in time, Columbia's top male stars were Melvyn Douglas, Richard Arlen, and Lew Ayers, none of whom had Grant's status as a leading man. The situation was a bit different at RKO, where the likes of Fred Astaire, Herbert Marshall and Robert Donat were very successful, but only in specific kinds of films (for instance, Astaire as a dancer in musicals), and lacked Grant's proven adaptability in multiple genres, from romance to light comedy to adventure.

Upon departing Paramount, neither Grant nor Vincent made any public announcements. They certainly didn't proclaim that the actor was going freelance. Instead, Vincent quietly worked the levers of power behind closed doors in the movie capital, seeking to land his client an unprecedented deal that would change the arc of Grant's career for the better. On February 5th, 1937 the motion picture trade newspapers reported that Cary Grant had just the day before, signed a contract with Columbia. The announcement lacked any details of the agreement, so the public assumption was that it was just another standard studio pact, locking up the actor in an exclusive deal, and subjecting him to the usual suspensions and term extensions to make up in the studio's favor for any suspended time which Grant may incur.

However, the deal was anything but standard by Hollywood's terms. There were three radical provisos. First and foremost, it was non-exclusive. Grant took seriously his decision to be a freelance actor, and that meant he wanted the liberty to work for anyone he chose.

Important as well was the salary, which saw him making a guaranteed $50,000 for each of his first two films[5], $75,000 apiece for the third and fourth and, should he and Columbia come to terms on an extension of the contract (which they did several months later), $100,000 per film for an additional four movies. Additionally, Grant had the right of refusal of any production which Columbia offered him, which meant that the studio could not suspend him for rejecting a role.

Last, but most definitely not least, Grant retained final say over any studio-released promotional material that featured him, so he was able to shape the public image he intended to convey, and steer clear of any of the inane publicity stunts which the studios routinely required their contract actors to engage in[6].

He in turn would provide his own attire for each film he made. This was not the hardship it may at first glance appear. Studio wardrobe departments didn't always keep up with the latest in men's fashions, and as someone who had long been carefully conscious of the clothes he wore, Grant wanted the fact that he frequently made the Hollywood 'Best Dressed Lists' reflected in his appearances on the screen. Furthermore, by using his own attire in his films, he could write off much of his everyday wardrobe on his income taxes as legitimate business expenditures.

Many in the press mistakenly announced that *When You're in Love* (1937) would be the first movie under this new agreement, primarily because it was released by Columbia just one week after the contract had been announced. But in fact, this had been another loan-out done while Grant was still with Paramount. The real star of the film was Grace Moore, who had been a soprano with the New York Metropolitan Opera, and whom Columbia had managed to establish as a popular, if mid-level, movie star. Her films were successful

---

5 Adjusted for inflation, this would come to $950,000 per film in 2022.
6 Quite likely, Grant was thinking specifically of the many photos which Paramount had staged with Cary and his friend, housemate and fellow Paramount contractee, Randolph Scott. Wishing to portray them as both rugged yet carefree, the studio had them pose stripped to the waist while working out and lounging together at poolside. All the photo shoots did was generate rumors that the two actors were having a homosexual affair. More on Grant and Randolph later in the book.

enough to help spark a fair interest in opera among Americans who might otherwise not have considered giving it a listen.

A romantic musical comedy, *When You're in Love* is perhaps most notable as the film in which Moore sang a version of Cab Calloway's "Minnie the Moocher", as well as for being the one and only directorial excursion of Robert Riskin, who had forged a highly successful screenwriting career in conjunction with director Frank Capra, resulting in such classics as *It Happened One Night* (1934), *Mr. Deeds Goes to Town* (1936) and *Lost Horizon* (1937). It was pleasant fare, and Grant earned many positive comments for his performance as the romantic interest, but it wasn't much better than the all-too-typical films he had been making for Paramount in his last couple of years there.

The first public inkling that Grant's new relationship with Columbia was anything other than the usual studio/actor accord came several months later, when the industry news publications revealed that Grant had just signed a virtually identical deal with RKO. This was unusual enough to get tongues wagging in Hollywood.

Yet even before he would start work with either Columbia or RKO, Cary Grant would be making his freelance debut working with independent producer Hal Roach.

High Spirits: *Topper*

The name of Hal Roach had been virtually synonymous with comedy in Hollywood for more than twenty years by 1937, having made scores of highly successful short films[7] starring the likes of Stan Laurel & Oliver Hardy, Harold Lloyd, Charley Chase, ZaSu Pitts, and the kids of *Our Gang* (1922 – 1944).

By the mid-Thirties, Roach was anxious to move beyond shorts and focus more of his efforts on the production of full-length features. His films had been distributed by Metro-Goldwyn-Mayer since 1927, but a decade later Roach was increasingly unhappy with them. MGM was more than willing to handle his Laurel & Hardy and

---

7   Shorts were films that had a shorter running time than feature films, usually anywhere between 10 and 40 minutes.

Our Gang productions, but there was little enthusiasm in Metro's Culver City offices for any full-length features from Roach that didn't star Stan and Ollie or Spanky and Alfalfa. The current distribution deal between them called for a Laurel & Hardy feature film in 1937, and two other musical comedies with other casts, with the option for an additional two features if the first pair hit specific profit thresholds at the box office. This was an imposed limitation on his creative expansion plans that Roach considered to be intolerable. In 1938, Roach would move his distribution to United Artists (and sell the rights to *Our Gang* outright to MGM, leaving shorts behind so that he could focus full-time on feature-length films.)

Until then however, the Hal Roach Studio had to deliver its products to MGM. Roach planned to maximize his limited resources by establishing separate internal features production units: one would focus exclusively on the Laurel & Hardy films, and the other on the remaining full-length films. Roach had intended to bring a former protégé of his, Leo McCarey, to run the second unit, but McCarey instead accepted a single film production offer from Columbia, so, starting with the second musical comedy of 1937 under the MGM pact[8], Roach chose as producer a young newcomer to his studio, Milton Bren. The film he was given to oversee was *Topper* (1937).

Published in 1926, *Topper* was written by humorist Thorne Smith. Smith had died in 1934, but *Topper* and several other of his works (including a sequel, *Topper Takes a Trip*) remained popular and in print, and in 1936 Roach optioned the movie rights to both *Topper* novels. He now turned to the first one in the hopes it would provide him with the box office success he desperately needed.

Topper tells the story of a staid, unhappy banker, Cosmo Topper, who is haunted by the ghosts of recently deceased friends, husband and wife George and Marion Kerby. Two madcap pleasure-seekers in life ... and in many ways, they can be seen as precursors of the 'screwball' film couples of the 1930s ... George and Marion find themselves stuck on Earth as ghosts after their accidental deaths in a car wreck, and they surmise that they need to do a good deed

---

8   The first to be released was *Pick a Star*, featuring Patsy Kelly and Jack Haley. Hitting theaters in May, it did not perform well at the box office, and its failure threatened to convince MGM to nix further Roach features. Therefore, this made the success of the second release all the more imperative.

for someone in order to earn their eternal rewards. They elect to pull Topper out of his rut and introduce him to a more exciting and happier life. Comic mayhem ensues.

Hired to direct was Norman Z. McLeod, who had gotten his start in Hollywood in the 1920s working in both animation as well as in shorts, before graduating to helming feature films. He had enjoyed tremendous success at Paramount in the early Thirties with a pair of Marx Brothers films, *Monkey Business* (1931) and *Horse Feathers* (1932), as well as *It's a Gift* (1934) with W.C. Fields. But several follow-up films did not fare as well, and eventually McLeod left Paramount in search of new opportunities to help rebuild his career. He landed at the Hal Roach Studio, where Roach appreciated the fact that McLeod's early work in shorts had taught him the art of getting a laugh in quickly and then moving on without lingering, which was exactly what the filmmaker wanted for *Topper*.

Roach and McLeod agreed on who they wanted for the three leads: W.C. Fields as Cosmo, Jean Harlow as Marion, and Cary Grant as George. Ill health precluded the first two from being cast; Fields was in and out of hospitals during that period for a variety of serious ailments, including pneumonia, an injured back, alcoholism, and depression. He would not be in good enough physical and emotional shape to step in front of a camera until months after *Topper* wrapped up filming.

Having starred in four films in 1936, Harlow had been dealing with exhaustion for several months, and was further debilitated by influenza, gallbladder ailments and, undiagnosed until later in '37, kidney failure. Desperate for time off to try and recuperate, Harlow asked her parent studio, MGM, to not loan her to Roach for *Topper*.

As for Grant, he was leery about the project. Supernatural fantasy films were often a hard sell to filmgoers; Alexander Korda's adaptation of H.G. Wells' *The Man Who Could Work Miracles* (1936) had been both a critical and box office disappointment, and surely Grant could not help but recall a film that he himself had participated in, Paramount's all-star *Alice in Wonderland* (1933), which landed with a resounding thud when it hit theaters. Given such uncertainty, the actor was reluctant to launch his new freelance career with such a dubitable effort.

However, Roach wouldn't take no for an answer. He and Grant were beachfront neighbors in Santa Monica, and the filmmaker often drifted over to Grant's place during the actor's Sunday open house parties. Sitting together at poolside, Roach argued that the film would be much more of a romantic screwball comedy than a supernatural story, and the script would be tailored to make the best advantage of Grant's proven comedic talents. And if that wasn't good enough, the $75,000 that Roach was offering him as his salary was definitely hard to pass up. After further consideration, Grant signed on.

He joined a production to which Constance Bennett had already been announced in the role of Marion Kerby. Also already cast was Cosmo Topper himself. With Fields unavailable, the part went to British actor Roland Young, who had campaigned hard for it. He had been a close friend and confidante of Thorne Smith during the last years of the author's abbreviated life (he had died at age 41 of a heart attack), and Young saw the opportunity of bringing the character of Cosmo Topper to life on the screen as a fitting tribute to his late companion.

Earlier in the decade, Constance Bennett had been the highest paid actress in Hollywood, making an unprecedented $300,000 for two films for MGM in 1931, and then earning a record-setting weekly salary of $30,000 from Warner Brothers to make a single picture, *Bought!* (1931). After a string of hit films such as *What Price Hollywood?* (1932) and *Our Betters* (1933), Bennett's popularity cooled, although by 1937 she was still demanding ... and receiving ... an impressive $40,000 per film (plus she secured top billing over her co-stars). That meant, between her and Grant, their salaries totaled more than one-fifth of *Topper*'s entire $500,000 budget. And while $500,000 would only narrowly elevate a film above 'B Movie' status at the likes of MGM and Paramount, for Roach it was the single most expensive production he had ever undertaken.

The main cast was rounded out with a trio of veteran character actors: Billie Burke as Cosmo's status-obsessed wife, Clara; Alan Mowbray as Topper's butler, Wilkins; and Eugene Pallette as Casey, a hotel house detective. Also among the players in smaller parts were Arthur Lake and Hedda Hopper (in one of her last films before she transitioned into a career as ultimately one of Hollywood's most influential newspaper gossip columnists). Uncredited bit roles were played by Ward Bond and, in only her second film appearance, 16-year-old Lana Turner.

The casting complete, Roach turned his attention to the script. Significant elements of Smith's original novel would have to be excised, due to their risqué nature, which would never have passed the Motion Picture Production Code. Roach wanted the laughs to be clever and to come fast and not dawdle before moving on to the next one, with a sheen of sophistication over everything; in short, a classic screwball comedy. Roach turned first to a familiar face on his lot, Jack Jevne, who had cut his teeth in the silent years writing comedy shorts for Mack Sennett, and in the sound, era had become one of the most prominent writers of Roach's *Our Gang*, as well as several Laurel & Hardy films. Jevne had been one of Roach's go-to writers for two recent Roach features, *Kelly the Second* (1936) and *Mister Cinderella* (1936). Jevne knew comedy, and he knew how to translate the comedic aesthetics of the shorts into a feature-length script.

Roach looked outside of his studio for the other two members of *Topper*'s screenwriting triumvirate. Eddie Moran's scripting roots also stretched back to the silent Twenties, and more recently he had written steadily for the long-running *Broadway Brevities* (1931 – 1943) series of musical shorts at Warner Brothers. Rounding out the trio was perhaps for many a surprising choice, Eric Hatch. Primarily a humorous short story writer and novelist, Hatch had only scant experience writing for films . . . but what little experience he did have is what sold him to Roach. Hatch had authored the book *1101 Park Avenue* (1935), which was adapted for the screen by Universal Studios as *My Man Godfrey* (1936). Universal hired Hatch to work with Morrie Ryskind on the screenplay, with the resulting film widely lauded for its sophisticated comedy and proving to be Universal's biggest hit of the year. Although it ultimately did not win any Oscars, it was nominated for an impressive six Academy Awards, including Best Adapted Screenplay for

Hatch and Ryskind. Adding Hatch to the writing team was a publicity coup and bolstered public anticipation for *Topper*[9].

In many ways as important to the film's success as director McLeod and the three screenwriters, was longtime Roach animation and process photography expert Roy Seawright who developed the film's optical effects. Considering the degree of special effects necessary to make George and Marion's ghostly antics appear believable on the screen, Seawright had to refine, and in some instances outright create entirely new, complicated visual tricks. His years spent concocting Rube Goldberg-ish props for *Our Gang*, as well as painstakingly devising the stop-motion march of the wooden soldiers in Laurel & Hardy's *Babes in Toyland* (1934), proved to be excellent training ground for bringing to life the hijinks of a pair of high-living spirits.

As *Topper* begins, the film wastes no time introducing us to the Kerbys and establishing their characters. We see the couple traveling down a country road during the night in their luxury convertible[10]. Marion is sunk low into the passenger seat, casually discussing how they had left a three day-long party at their own house, and they didn't even know who the guests were. George is sitting on the top of his seat, using his feet to steer the wheel, and is nowhere near the clutch, accelerator, or brake, casually singing a bygone folk song, "The Old Oaken Bucket." Both are relaxed, a bit wearied, and possibly a little drunk.

When Marion asks where they're going, George sings his response to the tune of "The Old Oaken Bucket," and his wife does a call-and-response:

George: "Oh, we're going to Wall Street to see old man Topper."
Marion: "Iron-bound Topper."
George: "That moss-covered Topper…that I promised to meet at his bank for the annual meeting of the board of directors at 10:30 in the morning."

With a giggle, Marion critically observes that those are too many words to sing. Then, since they have more than twelve hours until

---

9 Jeanie Macpherson worked uncredited on the original story treatment. Hal Roach himself doubtless made contributions to the script as well.
10 A 1936 Buick Roadmaster, modified to look like a Cord Phaeton.

the meeting at the bank the following day, we view a montage of the Kerbys visiting posh nightclubs in the city, finally ending after closing hours in a hole-in-the-wall Italian cafe, where the pianist (songwriter Hoagy Carmichael, making his motion picture debut) duets with them on his song, "Old Man Moon," as the flustered owner urges them to go home, and the rest of the staff are asleep. Still crooning the song, the couple finally wobble their way outside and climb into their car, where a milkman patiently stands waiting. Apparently, they have an ongoing agreement with him that he'll be ready with a bottle of milk for them when their evening revels finally end.

Thus, the first six minutes of the film establish that the Kerbys are clearly a pair of wealthy, fun-loving sybarites. The zany rich were a popular character type during the Great Depression, when presumably audiences with little or no money of their own could imagine happy-go-lucky lives for themselves through the figures on the screen. Roach, employing the storytelling economy of the shorts, has wasted no time in telling us all we need to know about George and Marion.

We then meet Cosmo Topper, and quickly discover that he's henpecked, and made to live his drab life down to the exact minute by his wife, who is terribly concerned about appearances. Indeed, we soon learn that Clara Topper is obsessed with social-climbing and believes that the key to enhancing their status is for her husband to be perfectly colorless and unworthy of gossip. Cosmo is clearly miserable living this way, but he submits to Clara . . . although he's not above grumbling to his secretary about it all. He's middle-aged but feeling much older, yet the kid inside of him took glee in having to dash to catch the train the day before, even if it did bring down a reprimand from Clara, who's aghast at the spectacle of her respected banker husband running through a train station like some mere clerk.

After the board of directors meeting (George is the single largest shareholder in the bank, but he displays scant interest in the institution's dreary details), Cosmo finds Marion lounging in his office. She proceeds to read him like an open book, observing that he's unhappy, and that his wife doubtless runs his life with monotonous precision. Clear by the way she lays across his chair is that she has also diagnosed his sexual repression, commenting that she guessed he hasn't had much fun in life for a long while: "I can tell that by the way you're staring at my knees."

George comes to collect Marion to depart, and he gives Topper a friendly caution: "Take my advice, don't let her make a guinea pig out of you. You'll never be the same again." As they head home George, who knows his wife all too well, warns her to not make a project out of Topper, reminding her that the last time she did something like that, it cost him $10,000 to settle. Yet Marion is now determined… but George is just as determined to get back to their home on Long Island, and he's driving faster than advisable. When something gets into his eye, he's momentarily distracted, missing a hairpin turn, and crashes into a tree, killing them both.

Their spirits rise from their bodies, wiping the dust from themselves as they wander over to a fallen tree to sit down, oblivious to the fact that they've died. It's only when they both notice the other is partially transparent…"Know something, George? I think we're dead."…do they fully realize what has become of them. When they don't "hear trumpets", George apprehensively asks, "What do you suppose is the conventional thing to do now?" With a sign, Marion responds, "I don't know, we've never been conventional."

Roy Seawright's trick photography is seamless here, and several minutes later we're treated to George (who's gone invisible so as to not "waste any ectoplasm") changing the car's flat tire, which is accomplished via wires invisibly lifting items and stop motion filming. The quality of the effects makes it fully possible for the viewers to accept that the Kerbys are, indeed, now ghosts.

The story continues to unfold at a rapid pace. Topper purchases the Kerby's repaired car, much to the chagrin of his wife, who dismisses it as a "painted Jezebel," and refuses to ride in it. In an act of defiance, Topper speeds off, but quickly discovers the burly auto is a bit too much for him to handle. After several near accidents, he blows a tire and only narrowly avoids crashing into the same spot where the Kerbys were killed. Shaken, he staggers over to the fallen tree, and is met by the materializing ghosts of George and Marion.

Realizing that in life they had a deficit of any good deeds, Marion guesses that if they can do such a deed now in their limbo state, they can earn their way into the great beyond. And that good deed is to turn milquetoast Topper into the kind of impetuous and fun-loving man he wants to be. During the antics that follow, the Kerbys get Topper arrested for drunk and disorderly conduct, and the story makes the newspapers. Humiliated, and believing that the scandal has ruined all hope of achieving her social climbing dream of being welcomed into the company of the eminent Mrs. Stuyvesant, Clara is soon astounded to discover that her husband's newfound notoriety has actually made him appealing to the uppermost crust of the social set, and Mrs. Stuyvesant invites the Toppers to her home. All seems well for the newly empowered banker.

However, more "help" from the Kerbys results in Clara accusing Cosmo of infidelity with a "fallen woman," sending Topper's life into a shambles. More hijinks ensue, and Topper is left comatose from yet another car crash, once again at the site of the demise of George and Marion. Cosmo's spirit says he wants to go with the Kerbys, "living on top of a volcano," but they assure him his life won't be so dull any longer and convince him to return to the land of the living, so that they can accomplish their good deed. Topper awakens the next morning in his bed, finding Clara determined to change her ways and save their marriage.

Through a long stretch in the second half of the film, George Kerby simply disappears from the story. This was done for the opportunity to play up the flirtatiousness between the teasing Marion and Topper. When George finally does return, he's in a jealous fit and hunting for Cosmo and his wife. He bedevils Topper at his hotel, startling multiple other guests and causing a near-riot, until finally Marion, highly pleased with her husband's jealousy and confident he truly loves her, suggests they kiss and make up. George happily agrees, cracking, "Hey, you know, this was the best fight we ever had!"

Grant was doubtless pleased by his character's inactivity for such a long a span of time, as it meant fewer days he needed to be on the set. Likewise, for the scenes in which George was invisible, Grant only had to have his voice recorded to dub into the film, so he didn't need to sit for makeup or work for hours under the hot studio lights.

Not having to be on the set every single day for long hours for weeks on end also meant that Grant didn't have to spend as much time in the company of Constance Bennett. It's a credit to the talents of both actors that their characters are so appealing together, because off-screen Grant found Bennett to be difficult, at best. By her own admission years later, she was a challenging presence on the set due to a combination of factors: fretting over the state of her career, which had gone into steep decline in recent years (just prior to making *Topper* (1937) she had been let go from her contract by MGM); her floundering marriage with French filmmaker Henry de la Falaise; her tumultuous love affair with actor Gilbert Roland; and dealing with the difficulties caused by the mental health issues and alcoholism suffered by her sister, Barbara. As a result, Bennett devoted her available energies to her performance, which between scenes left her coolly detached and seemingly indifferent to those around her.

That however was a rare downside to an otherwise positive filming experience for Grant. Much was riding on *Topper*; should it flop, it might be seen that he had made a colossal mistake by leaving Paramount. Columbia (and RKO) might even start to rethink having signed him and consider finding ways to conclude their contracts with him as expediently as possible.

His instincts told him to mine the comedy found in George for all it was worth. In this he was encouraged by director McLeod, who went so far as to allow Grant to improvise on camera in order to enhance a laugh. The result was a delightful performance that demonstrated on the screen as never before that Cary Grant had one of the deftest light comedic touches in Hollywood. The executives at Columbia and RKO took notice of that.

In this success he was ably abetted by his co-stars, Bennett, Young and Binnie Barnes; by the nimble direction of Norman McLeod; and by the excellent special effects of Roy Seawright. Even as the script tends to meander and bog down in the latter half of the film, all these other elements jelled to give *Topper* an irresistible momentum that carries it through to its happy ending.

The casting of Grant and Bennett proved to be a stroke of genius. As a couple, they provided both sexiness and glamour to degrees that few films of that era did (or usually could, given the restrictions of the Production Code). She moved with a feline poise, a saucy upturn on her lips, her designer gowns gracefully draped over her body as if she were a Renaissance sculpture. He gave living definition to 'Tall, Dark and Handsome,' once more the tuxedoed mannequin, yet now something much more as well, balancing his wit with a slightly dangerous air. In this film, Grant became perhaps the best amalgam of *The Thin Man*'s (1934) William Powell and *It Happened One Night*'s (1934) Clark Gable ever seen, yet he mimicked neither of them. He was in fact, for truly the very first time, pure Cary Grant...albeit still with rough edges.

Once filming concluded, Roach rushed the movie through post-production (he needed a hit, and he needed it *fast*). The film was released on July 16, 1937 to positive reviews and strong box office, thus properly launching Cary Grant's freelance career in splendid style[11].

❋❋❋

Those who saw *Topper* in theaters that summer could be forgiven for believing it was a Metro-Goldwyn-Mayer production. After all, didn't it open with MGM's Leo the Lion roaring Ars Gratia Artis? The average moviegoer didn't know very much about film distribution, exhibition circuits and such, so the fact that *Topper* was in fact produced by the Hal Roach Studio and only distributed by MGM would not have meant much to many -- but for Cary Grant, it was the closest he would get to four of the five major Hollywood studios for the foreseeable future.

---

11   The film was such a success, Hal Roach immediately commissioned a sequel, *Topper Takes a Trip*, adapting Thorne Smith's second and final Topper novel. Released only one year after the original film, the sequel boasted almost identical cast and crew credits with the first movie, with one very notable exception...Cary Grant did not return as George. Busy with other films, and uncertain about doing a sequel, he declined the role, appearing on screen only in a flashback sequence from the first movie. The sequel's opening credits proclaim, "Grateful acknowledgement is expressed to Mr. Cary Grant for his consent to the use of scenes from the original film *Topper*."

There is no evidence that most of the five majors ... Paramount, Metro-Goldwyn-Mayer, Warner Brothers and Twentieth Century Fox (with RKO being the fifth member of that quintet) ... officially blacklisted Cary Grant in his early freelance years. Indeed, Warners even inquired about having him star with Bette Davis in *Jezebel* (1938), only to balk at his salary demand of $75,000. Certainly, each of those studios had popular leading men of their own, and thus had less need of casting Grant than RKO and Columbia did.

Nonetheless, it seems unusual that Grant did *no* work at all for any of them for such a long time after having left Paramount. Nor is there any indication, beyond Warner's initial interest for *Jezebel*, that the four majors made any real efforts to acquire his talents at the time, despite his repeatedly demonstrated box office appeal. Paramount had had faith enough in him to so recently have offered Grant a lavish salary to remain on contract. Wouldn't it stand to reason that the studio would still want to avail itself of him from time to time?

There remains one very compelling reason why those four studios did not employ Cary Grant during these years, and it's the most obvious reason of all: they didn't want to start a revolution.

One of the bedrock strengths of the major studios was the contract system. Through it, they could control their talent. Oh, stars were still often truculent, but their binding contracts meant that studio executives could punish actors by suspending them without pay for weeks and even months on end (with the period of suspension added to the length of their contract, extending it beyond their original end date[12]), or banish them to do a lower quality film at another studio (just to remind them how good they really had it at their home studio). Contracted stars were required to be available to shoot films whenever and wherever their studio told them to. Stars could (and did) complain about the films they were being made to do, or the suitability of a particular director or co-star, or bring a grinding halt to a day's shooting over some perceived concern, often necessitating intervention from the highest echelon of the

---

12 In 1944, the California Supreme Court unanimously ruled in *De Havilland v. Warner Bros. Pictures* that the studios did not have the legal right to extend a contract beyond its established calendar years.

front office to resolve. Ultimately, in the final analysis, the contract system retained almost the entire balance of power in the hands of the studios, and they exercised it fully and without restraint.

But freelancing would fragment and erode that studio power. Actors would not be legally bound long-term employees, but rather independent contractors free to leave once a production was completed. They could reject any role they were offered, and they could take their talents to the competition. Thus, the studios could be assured that many of their biggest stars were paying close attention to what Cary Grant was doing, and if he succeeded, it might lead to the floodgates being opened all throughout Hollywood in due time.

The Hollywood moguls who ran the major studios saw the trail that Cary Grant was blazing and deemed it their road to ruin. They weren't about to help him pave it in gold by casting him in their films.

Love and Marriage: *The Awful Truth*

Almost immediately after filming on *Topper* had concluded, Grant had to report to Columbia for the first film under his new contract. And almost immediately after starting it, he had grave misgivings and wanted out.

Leo McCarey had learned his trade directing Laurel & Hardy shorts for Hal Roach in the Silent Era. With the coming of sound, he eventually found himself at Paramount, where he steered some of the studio's biggest comedy hits: *The Milky Way* (1936) with Harold Lloyd, *Ruggles of Red Gap* (1935) with Charles Laughton, and the film which many Marx Brothers devotees consider their masterpiece, *Duck Soup* (1933).

By 1937 he had parted ways with Paramount. Hal Roach was anxious to bring him back to his studio and offered him not only the directing chores on *Topper*, but also an executive producer role over other features. However, McCarey signed a deal with Columbia Pictures instead.

Columbia had for years been a mainstay of the so-called "Poverty Row," those smaller studios that didn't command the stars, directors or budgets of the major studios, nor did they own their own theater chains. The stock and trade of these small set-ups were low budget "programmers" and serials. But like the company's founder, President and production head, Harry Cohn, Columbia was as combative as it was cantankerous, and it literally slugged its way up to a position of eminence on Poverty Row, and then pugnaciously rose further still to forge a place for itself alongside Universal Studios and United Artists as a 'Minor Major' studio.

The key to Columbia's success ... beyond Cohn's relentless drive ... was director Frank Capra, who frequently in collaboration with screenwriter Robert Riskin had begun producing big box office hits. Columbia found itself elevated from its Poverty Row brethren when Capra and Riskin's *Lady for a Day* (1933) was nominated for the 1933 Outstanding Production (a.k.a. Best Picture) Academy Award, the studio's first such nomination. But if that was a home run for Cohn's studio, then Capra hit a grand slam in 1934 with *It Happened One Night*, the first film to win all five major Academy Awards: Outstanding Production, Best Director, Best Adaptation (for Riskin's screenplay), Best Actor (Clark Gable) and Best Actress (Claudette Colbert). Capra took a victory lap in 1936 with *Mr. Deeds Goes to Town*, which saw him win his second Best Director Academy Award. Each of these films were huge hits with audiences and gave Columbia the cachet to pursue bigger budgeted 'prestige' pictures.

But it was just such a prestige production that was causing mounting problems at Columbia now. The relationship between Cohn and Capra had always been tumultuous, but now they were openly feuding over Capra's current project, an adaptation of James Hilton's best-selling novel, *Lost Horizon*. Capra intended it to be an epic, and he convinced Cohn to set the budget at $1.25 million, far more than Columbia had ever spent on a single film. But as it turned out, as *Lost Horizon* (1937) drifted five weeks over schedule, and the director produced over a million feet of footage, the budget ballooned an additional three quarters of a million dollars, and with Cohn's blood pressure rising along with the dollars, this epic threatened to become a debacle.

When Capra turned in his finished cut, it was a staggering six hours long, and he suggested it be released in two parts. Instead,

Cohn ordered him to cut it down into a single film of manageable length, and Capra grudgingly edited it down to 3 ½ hours. Following a disastrous sneak preview, Capra cut nearly an hour more from the film, and even reshot some scenes in order to compress the story. By this point, he and Cohn were barely civil with one another. Much to Capra's ire, Cohn then took control of the final edit away from him and had another quarter hour of footage cut. The director was so enraged over this, he sued Columbia, and swore that when his current contract was fulfilled in 1939, he would never work for Harry Cohn again. Upon *Lost Horizon*'s release in the fall of '37, it was critically acclaimed and earned an Outstanding Production Academy Award nomination, but it lost money at the box office.

Earlier in the year, amid the swelling furor over *Lost Horizon*'s spiraling costs and production overruns, Cohn thought to put a scare into Capra by bringing another top director to Columbia, so as to get his resident prodigy to curb his excesses by realizing he could be replaced as the studio's premier filmmaker. Cohn's choice to fill this role was Leo McCarey, but what Cohn didn't realize was that McCarey and Capra were good friends, and when they quickly realized what the mogul was up to, they laughed over it. Capra encouraged McCarey to try and get the best possible deal out of Cohn and gave him his blessing to come to Columbia.

Negotiations between the studio and the director went well . . . until McCarey insisted that he would not accept any salary of less than $100,000 per film. Cohn, who was watching Capra's film hemorrhage his money, was looking to save cash, not spend more of it, and he refused. As McCarey got up to leave the executive's office, he knew he had one more card to play.

It was a scene so corny, it seemed straight out of a B-movie programmer: As he headed for the door, McCarey suddenly diverted to a piano that Cohn kept in his office, and he sat down. Everyone in Hollywood knew that before he got into movie making, Harry Cohn had been a Tin Pan Alley song plugger. In the early 20th Century, before the advent of radio, and when records were a rare luxury reserved for the well-to-do, new music found an audience when the tunes were performed by singers in vaudeville, burlesque, and in other musical venues. As more people heard the song, and liked it, they often bought the sheet music so that they could play it on an instrument in their own homes. That was how songwriters earned royalties on their work.

The job of a song plugger was to perform new songs for professional singers in the hopes they would add at least one of them to their repertoire. Young Harry worked relentlessly at plugging, never more so than when he championed a song that every other plugger had written off as a flop, "Ragtime Cowboy Joe." In no small part due to his Herculean efforts, the song went on to become a massive national hit, selling millions of copies of sheet music.

Although song plugging was twenty-plus years into his past, Cohn ... an otherwise hard-bitten grumbler ... held a sentimental streak for those long-ago days, and McCarey sensed that. Now as he sat at the piano, his fingers began to play the opening notes of an old standard, "Down Among the Sheltering Palms," a tune that McCarey had heard that Cohn greatly liked. The mogul came over to the piano, and the two men warbled through a rendition of the song. When they were done, Cohn told McCarey he could have his $100,000 salary.

The first project Cohn wanted McCarey to do was a film for Cary Grant, whom Columbia had just signed to an expensive contract. *Topper* had not been released yet, so the full breadth of Grant's comedic talent was yet unknown. But McCarey's specialty was comedy, and comedies were relatively inexpensive to produce (this film would be budgeted at $800,000, which was less than what Capra's *Mr. Deeds Goes to Town* had cost to make), so a comedy it would be.

The Awful Truth was by 1937 something of a warhorse in Hollywood. The 1922 play by Arthur Richman was successful enough on stage to warrant a film adaptation in 1925 starring Warner Baxter and Agnes Ayres, and another version in 1929, which featured Henry Daniell and Ina Claire. But the first was a silent film, the second a 'talkie', saddled with all the primitive technical drawbacks of those early forays into sound, with no modern version yet undertaken. Cohn currently had the film rights, and McCarey felt the story was ripe for an update.

When first approached about the film, Grant was apprehensive about the lack of even a preliminary script, but he respected McCarey as a filmmaker. Although they had never had the opportunity to work together during their concurrent tenures at Paramount, it was not for lack of desire on the actor's part. With the director's enthusiastic promise that the film would not only be a great comedy, but great fun for them to make, Grant agreed to do it.

Everett Riskin, the older brother of Robert, was initially assigned to produce the film, but accepted an associate position when McCarey insisted on producing it himself. Riskin had already engaged Dwight Taylor, who had written several of the Fred Astaire/Ginger Rogers musicals for RKO, to do the script for *The Awful Truth* (1937), but McCarey took him off the project (although he retained some elements of Taylor's screenplay). Instead, the director brought in a friend, novelist, and playwright Viña Delmar[13], to work with him on creating a new script from scratch.

At some point, Columbia also briefly assigned staff writer Mary C. McCall, as well as the writing team of satirist Dorothy Parker and her husband, Alan Campbell, to work on the film, but how much of their contributions, if anything, found their way onto the screen remains uncertain.

One change that McCarey could not make was in his leading lady, but in this he was more than happy to keep whom he had been given. It just so happened that McCarey and his wife were personal friends with Irene Dunne and her husband, and the director and actress had been hoping to find a project to do together. Dunne had enjoyed several years of box office success starring in both romantic melodramas and musicals, and then in 1936 she took the plunge into screwball comedy with *Theodora Goes Wild*. Critics loved it, and it was one of Columbia's biggest box office hits of that year. The role earned Dunne her second Academy Award nomination for Best Actress[14]. With Dunne having proven her comedic talents with *Theodora*, McCarey knew she had the ability to handle just about anything he could throw at her…and he intended to throw *a lot*.

---

13 Although Delmar is the only credited screenwriter of the film, the script is every bit a co-creation between her and McCarey.

14 The second of five throughout her career. For a good many years she held the record for the most nominations without a single win.

Cohn had contracted Dunne for a second film, with her own stipulation being that the film had to be shot during a specific window of availability for the actress in the summer of 1937. And even if the film wasn't made, Columbia would still have to pay her full salary of $40,000. Harry Cohn was determined to make certain he got his money's worth and the film got made, no matter what.

After Jerry and Lucy Wariner (the leading characters played by Grant and Dunne), the next character of importance is Dan Leeson. In Taylor's original script, Leeson was a dull and fussy Englishman, and the part was specifically written with Roland Young in mind. If Columbia could have foreseen the success that Grant and Roland would share just a few months later in *Topper*, it's possible that Cohn would have insisted they team up again for this film. However, McCarey wanted to change Leeson from a Brit to a Westerner, although he would remain just as dull, but now with a touch of hayseed in him.

Some have suggested that McCarey specifically made this change as a friendly tweaking of his friend Capra, as one could see some passing similarities between Dan Leeson and Capra's Longfellow Deeds from *Mr. Deeds Goes to Town*. Like Deeds, Leeson is good natured and a common clay type of man, very much a fish out of water in swank Manhattan. Both also share a passion for poetry. But whereas Longfellow eventually triumphs over his adversaries, Dan finds himself steamrolled.

Columbia assigned Ralph Bellamy to play Leeson, but when he was told there was no script available to read, he went to Cohn. The studio mogul admitted he wasn't happy that a shooting script wasn't ready yet, but he was trusting McCarey to come through when the time came. Still uncertain as to how to play his character, Bellamy next went to McCarey, whom he found to be friendly and welcoming, but nevertheless, "He wasn't helpful at all." McCarey had nothing to say about Dan Leeson and would offer the actor no advice on how to approach the part. At the very least, Bellamy asked in exasperation, could the director tell him what kind of clothes he should bring to wear? McCarey just smiled and suggested he bring a lot of different kinds of clothing, and they would figure it out later.

From the outset of McCarey's assignment to the project, chaos seemed to reign, although McCarey remained very much at the center of the vortex and was seemingly actively encouraging it as a necessary part of his creative process.

Harry Cohn expected his writers to work at the studio so that they were close at hand if he needed to see them. But Viña Delmar refused to even step foot on the lot, so she and McCarey either wrote together at her home, or else when they desired a change of scenery, they would drive over to Columbia, park outside the gates, and write from the front seat of the car.

All the same, once filming commenced, McCarey seemed to discard a good deal of what he and Delmar had written, and instead would spend the morning scribbling new lines, often on whatever scraps of paper he could find, and then assemble the cast and crew to shoot the scene. The actors, having only a scant amount of time to learn their new lines, were flummoxed … Grant in particular.

Grant's entire filmmaking experience had been within the structure of the Hollywood studios. That meant that the script would be ready in enough time for the actors to memorize their lines. Once on the set, they would usually rehearse a scene several times exactly as written, and then it would be shot. Everything was done on a strict timetable, and although films frequently did go over schedule, there was never any question that each day's work would begin at a set time, and work would continue uninterrupted until the scheduled end of each day's shooting.

Yet now here was McCarey, often letting his cast and crew sit idle each morning while he scribbled away at that day's pages, chuckling at what, as yet, remained his own private jokes. Or else he would sit at the piano on the set of Lucy's penthouse apartment, playing songs, largely to amuse himself. Even after a few productive hours of filmmaking, he often dismissed his cast and crew for the day at 3:00, rather than the customary 6:00 PM.

Cohn had informants everywhere, and he was growing increasingly exasperated by the reports he was getting about his expensive new director's work habits. Finally, he stalked down to the set, where he found McCarey entertaining the visiting Harold Lloyd. The mogul angrily barked that all visitors were to vacate the set immediately, and Lloyd departed . . . followed immediately behind by McCarey, who went home and refused to return to the lot until Cohn apologized to him, to the cast and the crew, and wrote a letter of apology to Lloyd.

To the astonishment of anyone who knew Harry Cohn, the studio head did just that, however begrudgingly. In spite of his frustrations with McCarey, he recognized that the director was something of a genius, and geniuses were invariably difficult. More importantly, McCarey had a track record of producing profitable films, and that was what mattered most to Cohn. The mogul could swallow his pride . . . at least this one time . . . if it meant getting a box office hit.

By the end of the first week, Dunne had gotten over her perplexity and was taking McCarey's eccentricities in stride, and Bellamy had concluded the director was a "comedy genius" and began thoroughly enjoying himself. But Grant was growing increasingly panicked, so much so that he finally wrote a memo to Harry Cohn entitled "What's Wrong with This Picture" and offered to pay Columbia $5,000 to let him out of the film. Shown the memo by Cohn, McCarey was so offended by his lead actor going behind his back this way, that he offered to kick in another $5,000 of his own money to be rid of Grant.

Cohn refused to release Grant. For one thing, it would have cost time . . . and in Hollywood time was money . . . to find another suitable actor. But furthermore, the studio head had seen the first few days of footage McCarey had shot, and he liked what he saw. Harry Cohn once famously said, "I have a foolproof device for judging whether a picture is good or bad. If my fanny squirms, it's bad. If my fanny doesn't squirm, it's good. It's as simple as that." And McCarey's film wasn't making his fanny squirm.

Things were tense on the set between director and star when filming resumed, but eventually the relationship improved between McCarey and Grant. In large part this was because Grant was finally grasping what his character was about, and he therefore became more comfortable in the role, and gave up the fear that he was ruining his career with this film. He was also greatly enjoying working with Dunne and Bellamy. Furthermore, the actor respected that McCarey encouraged him to improvise, as Norman McLeod had done on *Topper*, and the director was an appreciative audience for Grant's humor, often bursting out laughing at the actor's ad-libs. As filming continued, more than one person on set observed that Grant's performance as Jerry Warriner...charming, witty, warm, zany, somewhat devious...seemed to reflect more and more the personality of the film's director.

For his own peace of mind, Cohn made a point of steering clear of McCarey's set. But as the scheduled end of the shooting arrived, the mogul's curiosity got the better of him. To his chagrin, as he entered the sound stage one mid-afternoon, he found the director mixing cocktails for his cast instead of doing any filming. Cohn's temper flared, but McCarey instantly calmed him by announcing that they were toasting their completion...they had just shot the final scene. Not only had the director brought the film in on time, but he was $200,000 under budget as well! Cohn happily accepted a drink and toasted them all.

Only at this point was the method of Leo McCarey's madness obvious. His constant rewrites and the lack of a finished script was his way of keeping his actors mentally fresh and to prevent them from growing too comfortable (and bored) with the script. By frequently placing them off-balance, he knew they would be unable to fall back on any of their casual acting tricks and give anything less than a completely sincere performance. It also added a frantic air to the acting that bolstered the film's comedy.

The actors were often first learning each scene on the day they shot it. McCarey would rehearse them multiple times, but in a loose fashion, allowing Grant, Dunne and Bellamy to play around with the language and smooth it out in their own speaking styles, and of course welcoming improvisation. By the time it came to shoot the scene, the actors had creatively invested themselves into it, and they knew the scene's beats intimately, even if the dialogue might undergo some spur of the moment alterations. As a result, it was rare that McCarey didn't get what he wanted in the first take.

The film begins with Jerry Warriner returning home from a week's vacation in Florida. Except he wasn't in Florida, but rather secretly spent the week right there in New York City, staying at his club. We're supposed to believe that Jerry whiled away that time playing cards with his friends and just relaxing, but laid between the lines is the innuendo that he was having a liaison with a woman other than his wife. To fulfill his charade, Jerry spends time under a sunlamp to get a tan, and he also brings home a basket of Florida oranges; shortly after, wife Lucy notices that the oranges are instead stamped as having been grown in California.

Having invited friends from the club over to his place for drinks, Jerry is surprised to find that Lucy is not home waiting for him. He assures his guests that she must be with her Aunt Patsy, but the appearance of Patsy immediately quashes that idea. Then Lucy does arrive, accompanied by her handsome and suave music instructor, Armand. Startled to find Jerry home already, she explains that she and Armand had attended a music recital outside of the city the evening before, and their car broke down on the trip back, requiring them to spend the night at an inn until their auto could be repaired the following morning.

The guests (standing in for the viewing audience), aware of Jerry's vacation subterfuge, clearly assume that Lucy was taking advantage of her husband's absence to have an interlude of her own. In this, McCarey deviated somewhat from the original play, in which the wife's supposed infidelity was much less certain, and it was the husband who was considered the more likely guilty party. McCarey establishes firmly that Jerry and Lucy are a new kind of couple, and that she is a modern woman fully capable of pursuing her own sexual agenda, if so desired. Commonplace today, it was radical in 1937.

Neither Lucy nor Jerry believes the other, and things quickly escalate to the point where they agree that divorce is the best solution. The divorce itself is amicable, except when it comes to possession of their fox terrier, Mr. Smith[15], whom both wish to keep. Lucy enacts a bit of subterfuge in the courtroom to get the dog to come to her, and the judge awards her ownership, but with the stipulation that Jerry gets visitation rights.

---

15 Played by Skippy, a star very nearly as well known to audiences as Grant and Dunne, having found widespread fame playing "Asta" in *The Thin Man* (1934). At one point in *The Awful Truth*, Grant inadvertently calls the dog by his real name, instead of "Mr. Smith".

The courtroom scene was one of the few during shooting that required multiple takes, due to "Mr. Smith" not responding to his cues. Finally, Irene declared in mock exasperation, "Know what I think? I think that dog's gone high hat after playing with Bill Powell and Myrna Loy!" (in the *Thin Man* films).

With an interlocutory decree granted, so long as the divorce is not contested by either Jerry or Lucy within the next 90 days, it will become final.

A month later, Lucy is living in a new apartment with her spirited Aunt Patsy, who encourages her niece to go out and start enjoying life again, instead of just sitting around "moping." Patsy urges Lucy to get out that very evening, but her niece gloomily declines. Leaving the apartment and heading to the elevator, Patsy meets Dan Leeson emerging from the apartment across the hall. He's an oil fortune heir from Oklahoma, staying in New York on business, and sharing the apartment with his mother. Patsy and Dan enter the elevator as they continue speaking with one another; the doors close, and the arrow dial above the doors indicates the car is descending for several floors…until it abruptly halts and comes back up. The doors open again, and Patsy happily leads Dan back to her shared place, where she introduces him to Lucy. "He's a stranger in town," she tells her annoyed niece. "He'd take it as being right neighborly of us if we show him some of the bright spots."

Leeson, for all his good looks and polite manners, swiftly proves himself both a rube and a mama's boy. Asked what Oklahoma is like, he happily talks about his ranch, which is full of "cattle and horses and chickens and alfalfa." Lucy is just barely tolerating him, when suddenly there's a knock at the door.

Opening it, Lucy finds herself met by Jerry. "Well, if it isn't my ex," she says in surprise. The script had no line for Jerry to respond with, but Grant ad-libbed, "The judge says this is my day to see the dog." The crack broke up the other actors along with McCarey and stayed in the finished film.

Lucy introduces Jerry to Dan, and they shake hands, with the Oklahoman saying he's glad to know him.

Jerry: "How can you be glad to know me? I know how I'd feel if I was sitting with a girl and her husband walked in."

Lucy: "I'll bet you do."

"Don't mind me," Jerry assures the other three as he goes over to the piano to play with Mr. Smith. Suddenly mustering enthusiasm for Dan, she asks him to tell her more about Arizona, and he corrects her that it's Oklahoma. But as he talks, Jerry begins to pound out a song on the keyboard, drawing howls from Mr. Smith as they "duet" on the number. The racket makes it impossible for Lucy, Dan and Patsy to continue speaking. Irritated by Jerry's antics, Lucy declares that the three of them should go out for the evening and have some fun, her tone making it clear that she's doing this to spite her soon-to-be ex-husband.

As they stand in the hallway waiting for the elevator, Dan reveals that he's perhaps not quite the oblivious hick he's taken for, as he perceptively asks, "Are you sure you don't like that fella?" Incredulous, Lucy replies, "Like him? You saw the way I treated him, didn't you?" To which Leeson somewhat sagely responds, "That's what I mean. Back on my ranch, I got a little red rooster and a little brown hen and they fight all the time too, but every once in a while they make up again and they're right friendly." He has no idea how spot-on he is.

Having spent the night nearly 'til dawn nightclubbing, Dan tells his mother the next morning how smitten he is with Lucy and admits he may actually be in love. His mother is suspiciously dubious, assuming Lucy is just some big city fortune hunter trying to get her hooks into the Leeson wealth, and she tells him to forget about her. Meanwhile, Lucy is starry eyed about Dan, and confesses to Patsy that she's very fond of him. "He's sweet and thoughtful...sane and considerate. I was married to one who was insane and inconsiderate." Patsy is skeptical, warning her niece that Dan is just a rebound guy, and rebound relationships aren't made to last. "I didn't expect you to get silly about him," she says. Lucy asserts that she's completely over Jerry, and in fact she never loved him at all, and all she hopes is that Dan likes her as much as she likes him.

Presumably a few weeks later, we find Jerry at a nightclub, where he's sitting with his new girlfriend, Dixie Belle Lee, who works as an entertainer at the club. His mind drifts elsewhere as she talks to him with her honeyed Southern lilt, until finally he sarcastically asks, "How long have you been talking like Amos and Andy?" She smiles and says, "Oh, for quite some time. I got wise to the fact that it helps me in my work." Just then, Lucy and Dan enter the club. He's brimming with excitement as he says, "Just think of it, Lucy, you're going to be my wife!" But she's distractedly distant as she murmurs, "Yes, I am thinking of it."

The two couples meet on the dance floor, and Jerry insists they come to his table for drinks. Learning of their engagement, he acerbically needles Lucy by proclaiming his envy for the fact that they'll be living in Oklahoma City: "Lucy, you lucky girl! No more running around to nightspots. No more prowling around in New York shops. I shall think of you every time a new show opens and say to myself, 'She's well out of it.'" Impassively, Lucy says with little conviction, "I know I'll enjoy Oklahoma City," prompting Jerry to jab harder with, "If it should get dull, you can always go over to Tulsa for the weekend."

Soon enough it's Jerry who's squirming as Dixie Belle excuses herself to perform her number with the band. Called "My Dreams are Gone with the Wind" (written for the film by Milton Drake and Ben Oakland), the song starts out well enough, but the novelty aspect is soon revealed . . . along with much else . . . as at the end of each verse, a vent below Dixie Belle lets loose with a gust of air that blows her skirt up. The performance is an episode of exquisite bad taste, and all Jerry can do is to sheepishly say, "I just met her."

The next scene comically underscores the incompatibility of Lucy and Dan, as they sit at the piano in his apartment, duetting on "Home on the Range." Irene Dunne was a classically trained vocalist, and Ralph Bellamy was not. As Lucy sings, Dan warbles in a voice that's nowhere near in tune. But one discomfort for Lucy is replaced by another as Jerry drops in to discuss possibly selling his coal mine interests to Dan, and once more needles his almost ex-wife. As Jerry starts to leave, Lucy retaliates by surreptitiously tripping him, and Grant gets to demonstrate his talent for pratfalls, and not for the last time in this film.

Then, to demonstrate his love, Daniel reads a poem he has written for Lucy:

To you, my little prairie flower

I'm thinkin' of you every hour
Though now you're just a friend to me
I wonder what the end will be
Oh, you would make my life divine
If you would change your name to mine

It's all Lucy can do to not burst into laughter, and her efforts are hampered by Jerry, who unknown to Dan is hiding behind the door alongside them, and poking Lucy's ticklish ribs with a pencil.

But Jerry is not quite as over Lucy as he has tried to make it appear. The following day, certain that Lucy is off to an illicit rendezvous with her vocal instructor, Armand, Jerry arrives at the Frenchman's apartment. Barging in, he scuffles with the Asian butler in a jiu-jitsu tussle (and once again Grant displays his Pender-era acrobatic skills) before throwing open the door to the parlor, expecting to find Lucy and Armand in an embrace . . . and instead discovers that Lucy is giving a singing recital to a room full of very dignified looking guests. Embarrassed, Jerry sits down on a chair in the back of the room, leans back . . . and promptly crashes to the floor in a clatter. In a marvelous display of vocal prowess, Dunne seamlessly transforms the final note of her song into laughter at Jerry's haplessness.

Later relating all of this to Aunt Patsy, Lucy realizes that the only explanation for Jerry's crazy antics is that he's still in love with her. Only then does she admit her own truth: she's breaking off her engagement with Leeson, "because I'm still in love with that crazy lunatic, and there's nothing I can do about it."

She invites Armand over to enlist his help in convincing Jerry there was never anything romantic between her and the instructor. He gallantly agrees to aid her, but just then Jerry arrives. Realizing she can't let him see Armand there, she roughly shoves the Frenchman into a bedroom. Jerry has come to apologize for his behavior at the recital, and he sets his derby hat down on a table . . . not realizing that Armand's identical hat sits beside it, which Lucy quickly tosses aside to conceal it. But Mr. Smith, excited by his master's arrival and wanting to play, keeps retrieving the derby, while Lucy repeatedly hides it. When the dog once again returns it, Jerry prepares to leave and places the hat on his head . . . only to now discover that the derby is suddenly too large for him.

Before Jerry can determine what's going on, Dan and his "Maw" arrive. Realizing it would heap more embarrassment on Lucy to be found there with her, Jerry voluntarily rushes into the bedroom to hide . . . only to discover Armand already in there. As Lucy, Dan and Mrs. Leeson sit to talk, their conversation is increasingly drowned out by the sounds of a wild ruckus in the bedroom, with punches thrown and furniture smashed. Lucy tries to nonchalantly ignore it, but the Leesons are baffled by the mêlée. When asked what's going on, Patsy cracks, "Somebody's cleaning up in there." And then suddenly, Armand bursts out of the room at a full gallop, a furious Jerry hot on his trail as they dash out of the apartment. Dan and his mother are dumbfounded, Lucy is mortified, and Aunt Patsy sarcastically observes, "They forgot to touch second."

Convinced now that the rumors she had heard of Lucy's supposed infidelity with her music instructor are true, Mrs. Leeson imperiously stands up and instructs her son that they are leaving, thus terminating his engagement with Lucy. Dejectedly, the departing Dan tells Lucy, "Well, I guess a man's best friend is his mother."

Now free of Dan, Lucy finds she has also lost Jerry, who is more convinced than ever that she had been having an affair with Armand. They don't see one another for a few weeks, until Lucy opens a newspaper and learns that Jerry is engaged to socialite Barbara Vance, a "madcap heiress" who had set her sights on Jerry and snagged him. They engage in a whirlwind courtship and fill the daily gossip columns with tales of their jaunts to the polo games, horse races, and nightclubbing in Manhattan.

On the final day of their marriage (with the divorce set to go into effect at midnight that night), Lucy goes to Jerry's apartment to congratulate him on his impending marriage. Over a glass of champagne, she grows sentimental and recalls the first drink they had together, also champagne. Jerry toasted her that day with, "Lend me an ear, I implore you. This comes from the heart . . . I'll always adore you."

The phone rings, and without thinking about it, Lucy picks it up and answers. On the other end, Barbara demands to know who the woman answering her fiancé's phone is. Jerry takes the receiver from Lucy and, in a panic, concocts a lie that she is his sister, "Just got back from Paris." Still suspicious, Barbara insists that Jerry bring his sister to the dinner party her parents are throwing for them that evening. "Tell her I'd love to meet her," Lucy cattily informs Jerry. "Tell her to wear boxing gloves."

However, quickly realizing that this could be her last, best chance of winning Jerry back, Lucy concocts a plan. Convinced she isn't coming to the party, Jerry makes apologies for her absence, claiming she's still too tired from the ocean voyage. He then starts discussing his father, a Princeton man, "Class of '92." Jerry begins to regale the Vances with a tale of his father's football heroics against Yale.

He is interrupted by the unexpected arrival of his "sister," announced as Miss Lola Warriner. In walks Lucy, dressed as if for the burlesque, and speaking with a Southern accent that even Dixie Belle Lee would find over the top. She proceeds to undermine Jerry in the eyes of Barbara and her parents, painting a picture of him as a gold digger from a lowly background. She then mortifies the Vances by giving her own rendition of "My Dreams Are Gone With the Wind," prompting Jerry to finally lead her away as they make a hasty departure.

Lucy insists she must go to her Aunt Patsy's cabin, but thinking she's drunk, Jerry tells her she's in no condition to drive, and he takes her out to the country. On the way they're pulled over by two motorcycle police officers, and Lucy first convinces them that Jerry is drunk, and she then disables the car, forcing the cops to take them to the cabin on their cycles.

The caretaker is confused as to why they've come, since Patsy isn't staying there at this time. Lucy feigns surprise, but Jerry isn't buying it. Nevertheless, without his car, he has no choice but to stay the night. He and she are placed in adjoining rooms, with a door between them that conveniently has a broken latch, so that the night breeze coming through the window periodically blows it wide open.

As the clock ticks toward midnight and the legal dissolution of their union, each time the door swings open, we see that Lucy and

Jerry are still wide awake in their beds. And they engage in a conversation of doublespeak that nonetheless reveals much to the two of them.

Jerry: "In half an hour, we'll no longer be 'Mr. and Mrs.' Funny, isn't it?"

Lucy: "Yes, it's funny that everything's the way it is on account of the way you feel."

Jerry: "Huh?"

Lucy: "Well, I mean if you didn't feel the way you do, things wouldn't be the way they are, would they? Well, I mean things could be the same if things were different."

Jerry: "But things are the way you made them."

Lucy: "Oh, no. No, things are the way you think I made them. I didn't make them that way at all. Things are just the same as they always were, only you're the same as you were, too, so I guess things will never be the same again."

Just minutes before midnight, both Jerry and Lucy are anxious for the door to open again so that they can resume their discussion, but both are yet still too unsure of the other's feelings to open it themselves. Jerry even opens his window wider to try and push the door open with a larger gust of wind, but although it rattles, it won't budge, and he gets down on his hands and knees to try and peer under the door to see what's keeping it closed. What he doesn't know is that the house cat is laying against it on Lucy's side. When she finally spots the cat she shoos it away, and with his departure, the door swings open, revealing Jerry on his hands and knees.

Jerry then indulges in the film's supreme bit of nonsensical doublespeak as he confesses, "You're wrong about things being different because they're not the same. Things are different, except in a different way. You're still the same, only I've been a fool. Well, I'm not now. So, as long as I'm different, don't you think that, well, maybe things could be the same again? Only a little different, huh?"

Lucy casts a seductive gaze at him, and with that, Jerry secures the door shut with a chair, except he's now on Lucy's side in her room. The Hollywood Production Code forbade spelling out what came next, either in word or deed, so McCarey indulged in a touch of surreal whimsy to get the point across: he had been marking the passage of time in this final scene with a cuckoo clock that chimes every quarter hour, and in which we see two tiny mechanical figures, an Alpine shepherd and maiden[16], march out of separate doors, then turn around and go back inside the clock. As the clock announces midnight, the figures once more march out, except now the shepherd follows the maiden behind her door. Cue the end, with no doubt left in the minds of theatergoers that Jerry and Lucy have derailed their divorce through marital intimacy.

❋❋❋

Columbia released the film to theaters in major cities on October 21, 1937 and it was met with almost universal critical acclaim and ... most important to Harry Cohn ... robust ticket sales. In a year where Columbia was facing profit losses due in large part to the exorbitant costs and theatrical underperformance of *Lost Horizon*, *The Awful Truth*'s over $3,000,000 box office take helped keep the studio in the black.

Coming in the wake of the success of *Topper* (which had been released in July, amid filming for *The Awful Truth*), Cary Grant ended 1937 as more than just the boilerplate leading man that Paramount had reduced him to at the beginning of the year. He was a genuine star now. And more than that; he was a genuine *persona*. Like Clark Gable and James Cagney, he had fully established himself as a unique individual on the screen, so much so that from this point on, there could forevermore only be one Cary Grant-type in Hollywood, and it would be the original himself.

In addition to raking in millions of dollars, *The Awful Truth* was lionized by the press as an instant classic. Both *The Film Daily* and *Life*, along with many other magazines and newspapers, ranked the picture among their Top Ten Releases of the year (and in the case of *Life*, it was the only comedy to make their list).

The Academy Awards were no less lavish in their praise heaped on the film. *The Awful Truth* was nominated for six Oscars: Outstanding Production, Best Director, Irene Dunne for Best Actress, Ralph Bellamy for Best Supporting Actor, Viña Delmar for Best

---
16 It's unclear whether Grant and Dunne are playing the clock's figures, although they certainly bear a resemblance to the actors.

Adaptation, and Al Clark for Film Editing. The only one to take home a statuette was McCarey. He and Frank Capra, who had presented him the award, playfully tussled over the Oscar in a mock tug of war.

Most notable in his absence among the nominees was Cary Grant. While it wasn't unheard of for a lead actor to be overlooked in an otherwise heavily nominated film (in 1936, MGM's *The Great Ziegfeld* was nominated for seven Oscars, and won three: Best Picture, Best Actress, and Best Dance Direction, and yet, star William Powell was never even nominated for his role. He was however nominated as Best Actor for another film he did that year, *My Man Godfrey*, so he had some consolation.), in this instance Grant began to suspect his snub was intentional. The major studios still had tremendous sway over the Academy of Motion Picture Arts and Sciences, and it did not take much to make Grant suspicious that the more powerful studio heads were not about to reward the insolence of his freelancing by letting him get anywhere near an Oscar[17].

❦❦❦

At the time however, the rebuff by the Academy was a minor irritant at most. Everything else was breaking big for Grant. A week prior to the release of *The Awful Truth*, he signed another non-exclusive contract, this time with RKO Radio Pictures for $75,000 per film.

Although among the five largest and most powerful of the Hollywood Studios, RKO was in certain ways something of the odd man out. Unlike its rivals, its origins were not in silent films, but instead it was launched at the dawn of the "Talkie Era" specifi-

---

17 He held this opinion for a good many years, and even though he would be twice nominated in times to come for a Best Actor Oscar, he continued to believe that he was in essence being blackballed by the Academy. Eventually this would lead to a public estrangement between Grant and the Academy, which would end only in 1970 when he was presented with a Lifetime Achievement Academy Award. Still, it continued to rankle him that he was never rewarded for one of his performances, even as his films racked up Oscars for others. When Peter Stone accepted his Oscar for having co-written Grant's penultimate film, *Father Goose* (1964), he obliquely referenced the alienation between Grant and the Academy in his remarks: "My deepest thanks to Cary Grant, who keeps winning these things for other people."

cally to take advantage of the new sound phenomena. The Radio Corporation of America (RCA), a subsidiary of General Electric (GE), had developed an advanced sound-on-film process. Looking to expand its financial interests into film production, GE opened talks with a modest but profitable independent studio, Film Booking Offices of America (FBO), owned by banker and Wall Street broker Joseph P. Kennedy. They agreed upon banding together to create a new studio, with FBO delivering the film productions and RCA providing the new sound technology.

The third side of the triangle came from the Keith-Albee-Orpheum Corporation (KAO), possessors of one of the nation's largest circuits of motion picture and vaudeville theaters. At that time, what made a studio a major in Hollywood wasn't the number of films it produced in a year, nor the budgets it lavished on them. Acquiring status as a major came down to having the ability to distribute and exhibit your films. KAO gave the new studio ... named Radio-Keith-Orpheum (RKO) ... that all-important capacity.

Yet although by virtue of its production and exhibition arms RKO was one of the biggest players on the Hollywood field in the 1930s, it lacked a crucial element found at all the other studios: a nearly all-powerful mogul at the helm. Whether it was Louis Mayer at MGM, Adolph Zukor at Paramount, Jack Warner at Warner Bros., or Darryl F. Zanuck at Twentieth Century- Fox, each of those studios produced an aesthetic and style to their films that reflected the will of the man in charge. At least, that's what the public perceived.

Unlike the other studios, RKO never did ensconce a studio head who could exert such control over the studio's output. During Grant's five years at Paramount, next door neighbor RKO (their main studio lots were both on Melrose Ave. in Hollywood) ran through leadership tenures by William LeBaron, David O. Selznick, Merian C. Cooper, Samuel Briskin and Pandro Berman. What prevented each of them from consolidating their power and exercising fuller autonomy over the studio's productions was the fact that so much authority was kept by the corporate office in New York City. The result was the production heads often found themselves spending more time and effort battling the main office than taking a hand in guiding the films.

RKO rarely had topflight directors set down lasting roots at the studio, nor did they develop a signature star around whom they could build a consistent house style. The closest they came was with Katharine Hepburn, although her dramatic films gradually fell out of public favor. The duo of Fred Astaire and Ginger Rogers had produced a string of successful dancing musicals, but neither had yet really proven themselves as box office draws beyond that genre.

Nonetheless, RKO did have something of a house style, although it was less pronounced than the elegant gloss of MGM and Paramount, or the big city grit at Warner Bros, or rustic coziness at Fox. As most RKO theaters were located in metropolitan centers East of the Mississippi, much of the studio's output was tailored with an urbane sheen that appealed to Northern city dwellers. And the studio had a knack for turning out such unexpected hits as *King Kong* (1933), *Of Human Bondage* (1934) and *The Informer* (1935). Furthermore, RKO had the exclusive distribution rights to Walt Disney's cartoons, which all but guaranteed a steady stream of profits.

In short, RKO had great advantages, but also shortfalls that often prevented it from better exploiting those advantages. With the acquisition of Cary Grant however, the studio had hopes of bringing in a star around whom they could build a string of successful pictures ... and RKO wasn't going to wait.

They had already contracted months earlier with Grant for a single film, *Bringing Up Baby* (1938), which had begun filming in mid-September. Now, with Grant under a new non-exclusive contract, the studio announced several film projects scheduled for him: *Love and Parole* co-starring Miriam Hopkins, about which is recalled nothing; *Love Below Freezing*, a winter sports-themed romantic comedy with Ruby Keeler; *Irene,* alongside his occasional inamorata, Ginger Rogers; and *Joy of Loving*, which would re-team him with Irene Dunne. Of these announced productions, only the last one, retitled as *Joy of Living* (1938), would ever be made, although it would not star Grant and Dunne, but rather Douglas Fairbanks, Jr. and Ginger Rogers.

Whether Grant ultimately turned each of these roles down, or if RKO even had any intention of doing any of these films with him (it was not an uncommon practice for studios to announce impending films for their actors that they had no plans to actually make, just so as to get the names of their stars in the newspapers when there wasn't much else to say about them), the studio at the very least wanted to demonstrate that they were serious about making the fullest possible use of Grant. At least when he wasn't already tied up making a film for Columbia.

❋❋❋

As 1937 wound down, Grant could look back on perhaps his most momentous year since he first arrived in America. He had begun it by seemingly killing the golden goose in walking away from Paramount, and then surprised Hollywood by launching his Quixotic freelance career with back-to-back smash hits. And in those films, he at last established the on-screen persona that he had been cultivating since he had first stepped in front of a motion picture camera. The film he was shooting in those last months of '37 promised to be another success. It certainly was one of the funniest scripts Grant had ever read.

His relationship with Phyllis Brooks was growing more intimate, and he began to openly muse with friends about the possibility of marrying again. His tentative steps to reestablish a long-distance relationship with his mother were thus far complicated, but promising. And the charm he showed on the silver screen was very much in evidence in his real life, as he remained one of the more popular party guests in the cinema capital, whether it was at the chic galas thrown by the Countess Dorothy di Frasso, or the incongruous mix of formality and folksiness found at William Randolph Hearst's weekend gatherings at San Simeon.

The gossip columns routinely announced his attendance at racetracks, or the boxing matches. Movie fan magazines contrived the slightest of excuses to run his photos. He was now, in ways he never was before, a star.

 1938

"Mrs. Scott hasn't come between us at all. We're all as comfortable as ever."

If Grant's remark seemed odd when it appeared in the press, it was no odder than the relationship it referred to.

Cary Grant had first met Randolph Scott in the summer of 1932, when they both began working on the film *Hot Saturday*, and they immediately hit it off and became fast friends. The scion of a wealthy and prestigious North Carolina family, Scott had worked his way up from bit parts in Hollywood since his arrival in 1928, drawing comparisons to Gary Cooper thanks to his rugged good looks. Paramount finally took notice of him, and perhaps seeing him as a possible hedge against Cooper (as they had also viewed Grant), they signed him to a long-term contract.

Cultured, athletic and witty, he was in many ways the man that Archie Leach wanted Cary Grant to be. A few months after meeting, when Grant was looking for a new roommate to help him defray the rent of his Griffith Park home, Scott moved in. In 1935, silent film star Norma Talmadge's luxurious 5,500 square foot Santa Monica beach house became available for rent. Grant loved the place, but after a lifetime of thriftiness, he was reluctant to foot the pricy monthly bill. Besides, now that he had divorced Virginia, he felt the place was too big for him alone, and Scott suggested they continue their living arrangement, with the two of them splitting the bills.

Paramount was pleased with this arrangement, as it gave them a unique public relations angle to promote their two contract players. Filling the movie magazines were photos and stories of the two 'carefree bachelors,' all of them carefully staged by the studio. Female fans certainly appreciated the pictures of the two muscular stars minus shirts as they worked out or swam in the pool – but then the whispers began.

Photographs of the two actors smiling at one another across the breakfast table or cooking together in the kitchen (with Grant wearing an apron) appeared to some to project a much less masculine image than Paramount had intended. For a few, it wasn't a great leap of logic to make. In some quarters, the acting profession was believed to be rife with homosexuality. Furthermore, there was a widespread, antiquated and utterly unsubstantiated notion that British men tended toward homosexualism (this was most prevalent in the American Midwest, where few natives had an opportunity to ever actually meet someone from Great Britain). Given that Grant was both British and an actor, doubtless some took it as an article of faith that he preferred the company of men over women. Seeing some of the pictures taken with Scott, it's no surprise that rumors began to crop up.

The Tijuana Bibles didn't help matters any. Those were crudely drawn pamphlets printed on cheap paper in wallet-sized dimensions, and they were most definitely *not* for children. Usually, they were eight-page cartoon stories featuring celebrities or comic strip characters in lewd and unsubtle sex acts, available for purchase under the counter in less reputable cigar stores and other seedy establishments, and widely passed around among friends. Frequently the male actors featured in Tijuana Bibles were depicted as homosexuals, Cary Grant among them.

Doubtless the rumors found their way back to Grant and Scott, but neither would acknowledge them publicly, nor could they. Homosexuality was a taboo subject for public consumption in that era, and in fact was almost never discussed in the press. When it had to be brought up in so-called polite company, the common euphemism for the practice was "family life," and practitioners were dubbed "temperamental." In California in the 1930s, homosexuality fell under the criminal code for sodomy, and could result in up to fourteen years in prison. Furthermore, the state had the right to sterilize those convicted for such "perversion."

Even a marriage couldn't still the whispers. In fact, it made them worse.

In 1936 Scott married Marion duPont, an heiress of the chemical company, and a prominent thoroughbred horse breeder. In March of that year, Scott had returned home for the funeral of his father, where he reconnected with duPont, a childhood friend. After a whirlwind courtship, they secretly wed, and kept their nuptials undisclosed for several months. When they finally announced it to the press, their marriage filled the society pages of newspapers across the country, but what raised eyebrows was the new Mrs. Scott's declaration that she had no intention of living in California, and she decamped for Virginia, where she owned and resided in Montpelier, the home of the fourth U.S. President, James Madison. As her husband's work required him to reside in Southern California, he continued to room with Grant in Santa Monica the same as before. She rarely ventured West, so Scott had to travel to Virginia between film shoots to visit with his wife.

Not surprisingly, the unconventional habitations of Mr. and Mrs. Scott aroused comments. For those who knew Randolph Scott, they understood the circumstances. He was not about to give up the career he had worked so hard to build and which had become so central to his sense of identity, nor was he comfortable in Marion's world of pomp and formality, despite his own affluent upbringing, and to friends, it made perfect sense that Scott continued to live with Grant. Each found the superficial bonhomie so typical in Hollywood to be distasteful, and distrusted many who tried too earnestly to gain entry into their small social circle. Add that Grant and Randolph deeply liked and, just as importantly, trusted one another, and as both men attempted to navigate the treacherous shallows of the motion picture industry, knowing they had someone watching their back was a comfort worth its weight in gold.

Scott did not seem to be lonely without his wife in California. According to many who knew both men, Grant and Scott were rarely alone when at home. There was a steady stream of women who traveled in and out of their bedrooms at the house on Palisades Beach Road[18].

---

18 To answer the question so frequently asked…were Cary Grant and Randolph Scott in a sexual relationship?…all this author can say for certain is, there is no answer. All we do know is that none of Grant's nor Scott's close friends or relatives have

As for Randolph and Marion Scott, they continued to live apart until finally divorcing amicably in 1939.

●●●

'Til That Lucky Day: *Bringing Up Baby*

Howard Hawks was an exceptionally successful director, having turned out such box office hits as *The Dawn Patrol* (1930), *Scarface* (1932) and *Ceiling Zero* (1936), among others. He had helped pioneer the screwball comedy film with *Twentieth Century* (1934), and he was ready to return to the genre at last.

RKO had purchased the film rights to "Bringing Up Baby", a short story by Hagar Wilde that had run in *Collier's Magazine*. Wilde was also contracted to help write the screenplay, along with veteran screenwriter Dudley Nichols. The studio had specifically purchased the story for Katharine Hepburn, who despite continuing to receive critical accolades for her performances, had seen too many of her recent films...*Quality Street* (1937), *A Woman Rebels* (1936) and of course *Sylvia Scarlett* (1935) wither and die at the box office. Although her *Mary of Scotland* (1936) had done well financially, that wasn't enough to deter the President of the Independent Theater Owners of America, Harry Brandt, from declaring her "Box Office Poison" for 1938[19], a potential kiss of death for her career as a leading lady. Since her dramatic roles were no longer attracting customers, RKO reckoned, they may as well try her in a comedy. After all, they had nothing left to lose.

With the addition of Hawks as director, the film officially became a major production for the studio. Hawks threw himself into working on the script alongside Nichols and Wilde, and the story went from being a romantic comedy to something wilder and more unrestrained, a true apotheosis of screwball.

The initial difficulty was in getting a suitable leading man to play opposite Hepburn. The studio's top choices for the role, Leslie

---

ever claimed they were, and several of them have strongly asserted that the rumor is simply not true. Ultimately of course, it simply doesn't matter.

19 Hepburn was in good company. Other actresses on the list included Greta Garbo, Joan Crawford and Marlene Dietrich.

Howard, Fredric March and Robert Montgomery, all declined. So, when Frank Vincent came calling to discuss finding a film project for Cary Grant, RKO was more than interested.

At first glance, Grant would seem to be all wrong for the male lead in *Bringing Up Baby*. His character, Dr. David Huxley, was a milquetoast intellectual, repeatedly baffled and overwhelmed by Hepburn's Susan Vance…a far cry from any role Grant had played before, and certainly the opposite of the fast-talking, witty and sophisticated persona he had been establishing with *Topper* and *The Awful Truth* in 1937. What's more, Grant most definitely did not look the part. Even beneath a suit and tie, his broad shoulders and barrel chest could not be hidden. Given his physique and his dashing good looks, one would have to wonder just how in the world David Huxley became so meek and maladroit, particularly around women. It was a part seemingly tailor-made for the likes of Henry Fonda (who would go on to play a not-dissimilar character in 1942's *The Male Animal*) but seemed a far cry from Cary Grant.

What's more, Grant knew it, and had initially rejected *Bringing Up Baby* because of this. But Hepburn very much wanted to work with him again, so she and her boyfriend, millionaire industrialist, aviator and occasional film producer Howard Hughes (who was also a good friend of Grant's), paid him a visit at his home and after a spirited discussion, convinced him to take the part (after Frank Vincent negotiated a $75,000 fee, that is).

Hawks was happy that Grant was aboard, believing all along that he was the perfect choice, but he knew he had to convince the actor he hadn't made a mistake in agreeing to do the film. It was clear to Hawks that the only way that Grant could carry off this part would be by giving a performance that made viewers forget his looks and focus solely on his delivery. And the director knew just how to accomplish that.

Harold Lloyd had been, along with Charlie Chaplin and Buster Keaton, one of the most popular and influential comedians in silent pictures. He still made occasional sound films but was more or less retired from acting by 1937. When Grant came to Hawks and asked him how he should play his character, the director simply said, "Like Harold Lloyd," and according to Hawks, Grant instantly understood and completely grasped who David Huxley was. Having been a big fan of Lloyd's work back in the Twenties, Grant relished the opportunity to invoke his style in this film. He even donned a pair of Lloyd's signature round glasses for the part, and consulted Lloyd himself on how to play certain scenes.

Katharine Hepburn did not find it quite so easy to understand how her character should be played. Having no experience doing comedy, she approached it much as she would a dramatic part, investing far too much exuberance into her performance. The result was anything but comedy, but rather a too-earnest effort that fell flat; an actress attempting to act funny, rather than just being funny.

But Hawks had a solution for her as well, although it required more than simply invoking a famous name. As he recollected years later, "I couldn't do anything with her. So I turned to an actor, Walter Catlett, who had been a comic in the Ziegfeld Follies, and I said, 'Walter, have you been watching Miss Hepburn?' He said, 'Yeah.' 'Will you tell her what she is doing wrong?' 'Nope,' he said. 'Will you tell her if she asks?' I asked. 'I guess I would have to,' was his reply." Hawks introduced Hepburn to Catlett, and they went off for a chat, during which he explained the secret to successful comedy; basically, a funny line of dialogue only works if you take it seriously. It was a revelation to Hepburn, who requested that a larger part be written into the film for Catlett, so that he could remain handy on the set when she needed more of his guidance.

Hawks insisted to the writers (and he himself did a good deal of uncredited work on the script) that the story should not be too plot-heavy, that rather the comedy should carry the scenes. At its core it is an about-face from the typical Boy-Chases-Girl tale, with the man in this instance being the pursued party, and the woman pulling him into increasingly madcap situations in her pursuit of him. In the dynamics of film comedy, he's the straight man, and she's the clown.

The film introduces us to David Huxley, a shy, self-conscious paleontologist whose life is devoted to completing a fully intact skeleton of a brontosaurus, for which he only needs one more bone, the intercostal clavicle[20], scheduled to arrive soon. He is engaged to be married to his assistant, the sternly dispassionate Alice Swallow (played by Virginia Walker), who feels her duty is to marry David so that she can make certain he continues to carry out his life's work without distractions. "Nothing must interfere with your work," she austerely informs him when David tries to peck her cheek. "Our marriage must entail no domestic entanglements of any kind." Hearing this, David sheepishly asks if 'domestic entanglements' include children as well, and Alice sweeps her arm out toward the massive skeleton and announces, "This will be our child."

The museum needs a million-dollar endowment from the wealthy Mrs. Elizabeth Random to finish financing David's exhibition, and so he goes to play golf with her attorney, Mr. Peabody, on whose recommendation the endowment hangs. At the golf course he inadvertently meets Susan Vance, a flighty, free-wheeling young woman, when she carelessly plays his ball. It turns into an exasperating experience for the proper and logic-driven David, and he is happy to finally be rid of her... but then as she tries to depart from the country club, she hits his car bumper with hers, locking them and throwing David into a tizzy. The incident ruins the game with Peabody and puts the endowment in jeopardy.

Naturally enough they meet again, and Susan drags David through a progression of misadventures that steadily tear away not only his dignity, but also his reticence. In a hotel cocktail lounge, where David has gone to apologize to Peabody, Susan is also there, and her mischief gives Grant a chance to indulge in a pratfall. His self-respect is further demolished by having his top hat flattened and his dinner jacket torn. But the tables are quickly turned when the back of Susan's skirt is accidentally torn away by David without her knowledge. As she walks away, David follows her closely behind in lock step to preserve her modesty, much to the amusement of onlookers.

Based on no real evidence whatsoever, Susan has concluded that David has a romantic fixation with her, and she likes it. One can practically see the wheels turning behind her eyes as she determines

---

20 This was entirely an invention of the writers. There is no such thing as an "intercostal clavicle".

to win him. Her means of doing so is to plunge David's well-ordered life into total chaos.

The "baby" invoked in the film's title reflects not only the brontosaurus skeleton, but also Susan's pet leopard, whom she named "Baby". She also has a pet terrier, George, played by Skippy (who had of course just recently worked with Grant in *The Awful Truth* {1937}). As circumstances unfold, George steals the intercostal clavicle and buries it. David accompanies Susan to Connecticut along with Baby, who then escapes. With an utter lack of probability, another leopard, this one dangerous, has also escaped from a circus in the area, leading to confusion and mistaken (feline) identity. Adding to the lunacy, Baby can only be lulled by hearing the song "I Can't Give You Anything but Love, Baby", which Susan and David dutifully croon in a bid to lure the leopard down from a rooftop.

As the story careens down its twisted path, David has lost his clothes, and the only thing Susan has for him to wear is a frilly negligee. Naturally, he is then discovered by Susan's Aunt Elizabeth (a.k.a. the Mrs. Ransom who is considering endowing David's work), played by May Robson, and when she inquires why in the world he's dressed that way, his exasperation erupts and he snaps, "Because I just went gay all of a sudden!"

The penultimate scene is a comedy of errors in which both Baby and the dangerous leopard are brought to the local jailhouse, and David saves Susan from the killer cat by luring it into a jail cell, during the process of which she confesses her love for him. With the leopard safely locked up, David promptly faints[21].

The film approaches its finish back at the museum as we see an indignant Alice breaking off her engagement with David, accusing him of being a "butterfly" (by which we assume she means frivolous and undependable, which are doubtless cardinal sins in her book). She stalks off, leaving him behind. Just then, Susan bursts into the room, holding the intercostal clavicle in her hand, explaining that she followed George around until she caught him digging it up.

---

21 The fainting bit was a last-minute change. Originally, David was supposed to say to Susan after the danger passes: "Susan Vance, you're a menace to society. I never want to see you or your aunt or your panther again! I'm going back to my museum, and I'm going to be quiet!"

David rushes up to the top of the scaffolding next to the skeleton, reluctant to come down, fearful of what chaos may erupt should he get too close to Susan again. "Put it down on the table and go away!" he pleads. But she refuses, then starts to climb a ladder to come up to him, despite his protestations, cheerily telling him that her aunt will still donate the million dollars to the museum.

In the original script, trying to convince her (and himself) that their relationship couldn't possibly work, David proclaims, "There is a difference between science and love. I am devoted to science; you are devoted to love." As she reaches the top of her ladder, it begins to sway wildly from side to side, until she must clutch a rib of the brontosaurus to not topple to the floor. But her weight proves too much for the fragile structure, and Susan falls with the dinosaur, buried beneath a pile of its bones. David rushes down and frantically digs her out of the wreckage, and is relieved to find she's only stunned, not injured. He cradles her and says, "Darling, this is going to be terrible…but will you marry me?" The end and fade out.

Hawks however had changed his mind about that ending when the time came to shoot it. Having gotten a taste of Grant's acrobatic prowess earlier in the shoot, he decided to make use of it now. He suggested that when the skeleton collapses, Grant should grab Hepburn's hand and pull her up to safety. The actress wasn't particularly thrilled with that idea. Although athletic herself, and often willing to undertake her own stunts, this one smacked of being overly risky. There would be nothing to save her from a twenty-foot fall to the studio floor, save for her co-star's reflexes and strength – and there would be no way to properly rehearse the new scene, because the skeleton was not designed to be quickly reassembled after collapsing. Grant liked the new idea and assured her that she would be perfectly safe. He showed her a tumbler's trick: clutch the wrist, not the hand, so that your grasp doesn't slip.

With the cameras rolling, Hepburn made her way up the tall ladder. Susan apologizes to David, but he surprises her by excitedly replying, "Why, I ought to thank you. You see, I've just discovered that was the best day I've ever had in my whole life!" Hardly believing what she's hearing, Susan says, "But…*I* was there!" David just smiles and responds, "Well, that's what made it so good!" Elated to hear this, Susan blissfully starts to rock from side to side, the ladder swaying like a metronome. When both then realize her predicament, she frantically jumps from the ladder onto the back of the brontosaurus, but that causes the entire structure to collapse. True to his word, Grant firmly took Hepburn by the wrist and with seemingly little effort, hauled her 125 pounds up onto the scaffolding with him.

As they sit side by side, he tries without success to get a word in edgewise, as Susan exclaims, "David, can you ever forgive me? You can! And you still love me! You do! Oh, David!" Realizing that trying to reply is a fruitless battle, he simple throws his arms around her and they embrace.

* * *

There were a lot of things about *Bringing Up Baby* that made RKO unhappy. First there was the initial $750,000 budget, which was more than the studio wanted to pay for a Hepburn vehicle, given the losses many of her more recent films had racked up. Grant's $75,000 salary (Hepburn was getting the same) contributed to that high price tag. Having to construct from scratch a full-sized (twenty feet tall and sixty feet in length) brontosaurus skeleton didn't come cheap, either, but as it turned out that planned budget came and went, as Hawks ... a notoriously slow director ... stretched filming from the scheduled fifty-one days to nearly double that, ninety-three days, necessitating a budget increase to over $1 million. Thanks to a provision in his contract, since the shooting ran over-schedule, Grant got a salary increase of some $50,000 above his $75,000. At that rate, even if the film proved to be a box office match for any of Hepburn's most successful past pictures, it would turn only a small profit at best. On the other hand, if it did as well as *The Awful Truth*, RKO would be swimming in greenbacks.

The studio was also nervous about Cary Grant. They disliked the pair of glasses he wore, arguing that they diminished the movie star good looks RKO was paying dearly for. Also, what was the deal with the mincing and unassertive characteristics he played his role with? Additionally, when he got mad, why did he whinny like a horse? Sure, the dailies made it plain that the film was funny, but the studio executives still fretted that this was a motion picture that would have to work hard to find its audience.

Hawks ignored the increasingly urgent demands from the front office to hurry up and finish the film, and continued to make it as he saw fit, on his own timetable. He, like Leo McCarey and Norman McLeod, also encouraged improvisation from the actors. In one instance, when the heel of Hepburn's shoe unexpectedly broke off during a scene, throwing her walking askew, the quick-witted Grant whispered to her, "I was born on the side of a hill." Hepburn promptly spoke the line aloud, and it cracked everyone up . . . a lot of takes were spoiled by spontaneous laughter among the cast and crew . . . and Hawks instantly ordered it written into the script.

While Grant was unafraid to take a pratfall, or save Hepburn from falling to her demise, he drew the line at working with the leopard. Although the jungle cat, named Neissa, was tame and trained, Grant had seen enough "tame" animal acts back in his vaudeville days to know that animals from the wild can never be fully trusted. As a result, in most of David's scenes with Baby, they were not actually together, but rather their proximity is the result of split screen optical effects, or else he's working with a lifelike stuffed doll (which Hepburn used to terrify Grant one day by dropping it onto him from above). Hepburn had no such reluctance to work with Neissa, and would often stroke the leopard's fur, while the cat would occasionally nuzzle against her thigh, but events almost took a frightful turn one day when the clinking of wardrobe weights woven into Hepburn's skirt startled the cat. It was about to pounce on her, fangs bared, when the trainer, Olga Celeste, suddenly jumped between the animal and the actress and began cracking her whip to drive the leopard back. Afterward, Hepburn made a point of always approaching Neissa with considerable caution.

* * *

RKO wanted the film in theaters as soon as possible, to strike while the iron was hot. During the filming of *Bringing Up Baby*, the studio had released *Stage Door* (1937), an adaptation of Edna Ferber and George S. Kaufman's hit Broadway play. Although Katharine Hepburn had top billing, the cast was as close to an all-star ensemble as RKO could muster, with Ginger Rogers and Adolphe Menjou headlining along with Hepburn, and Lucille Ball, Eve Arden and Ann Miller in supporting roles. *Stage Door* was a tremendous hit, earning nearly a million dollars in box office profit, thus making the charge that Hepburn was box office poison seem ill-considered. What would make it entirely ridiculous and forgotten however would be an immediate follow-up hit.

Because they were so deeply over schedule, Hawks and his editor, George Hively, had begun cutting and editing the film while it was being made. They even invited Grant along to get his opinions on how to present certain scenes. As a result, Hawks turned in a finished cut to the studio, clocking in at 112 minutes, just days after the last scene was shot. Several sneak previews were held in Southern California that January, earning hearty laughter and rave reviews from viewers. Hawks took the film back and trimmed an additional ten minutes from the length, tightening the already rapid-fire pace even more, and *Bringing Up Baby* made its official premiere on Wednesday, February 16 at the RKO Golden Gate Theatre in San Francisco. Initial critical reaction was highly positive, such as the review from *The Hollywood Reporter*, which congratulated the film for striking "a high note of hilarity," and cited the "high quality cast which obviously enjoyed itself hugely in the making thereof." The reviewer specifically highlighted Grant and opined that his "work in this role should make him stronger than ever."

Over the next several weeks the film debuted in various cities, steadily moving eastward, and drew strong business in Los Angeles, St. Louis, Chicago, Detroit and Boston. Then a curious thing happened. Just as the movie opened at the Radio City Music Hall in New York City, *New York Times* film critic Frank S. Nugent panned the film, dismissing it as "a zany-ridden product of the goofy farce school." Other Northeastern critics, seemingly taking their cues from the *Times*, then began giving the film, if not outright bad reviews, mixed ones. During its first week at Radio

City, *Bringing Up Baby* did $70,000 at the box office, which was not a terrible draw, but still not enough to warrant holding it over for a second week. Overall, the film did weak business in New York City and its environs, which then seemed to reverberate across the nation, with the early strong box office swiftly diminishing, as word of mouth about the poor reviews appeared to overtake the praises of any who had actually seen and liked the movie.

Had the production not exceeded its original budget, it would have enjoyed a solid profit of some $300,000 or so, but because it was so vastly over-budget, it lost money during its 1938 theatrical run (re-releases in the 1940s finally saw the film earn enough to turn a small profit). Perceived as a "flop", the underperformance of *Bringing Up Baby* led to several momentous decisions at RKO.

The film's first casualty was Katharine Hepburn. RKO was now done with her, convinced she no longer had a commercial future in Hollywood. She was still contracted through the end of 1939, but RKO offered to let her buy herself out of her contract for a staggering $200,000. To induce her to accept the deal, they informed her that her next production would be a B-film titled *Mother Carey's Chickens* (1938). Hepburn had no difficulty reading the writing on the wall: RKO would scuttle what was left of her career in a string of inferior films unless she paid them off and went away. Grant advised her to do just that, encouraging her to go freelance just as he had done. She paid RKO's fee and walked out of their Gower Street gate for good.

Next on the chopping block was Howard Hawks. Although *Bringing Up Baby* was only the first of a multi-picture agreement he had recently signed with RKO, his inability to stay on-schedule and on-budget was alarming. The fact that the end result failed to turn a profit was inexcusable. The studio tore up his contract and let him go.

About the only principal figure in the creation of *Bringing Up Baby* to escape unscathed was Cary Grant. RKO simply concluded they had chosen the wrong vehicle for him, and that its failure wasn't his fault. The successes of *Topper* and *The Awful Truth* demonstrated his box office vitality, so the matter just came down to picking the correct role. The studio would busy itself in that task in the coming months. Meanwhile, the actor would now head back to Columbia for his next picture for Harry Cohn.

●●●

All the Faith in the World: *Holiday*

There's a certain irony that the film which Cohn had lined up for Grant was an RKO cast-off, purchased by Columbia back in 1936 when RKO was selling some story properties in order to raise cash. Philip Barry's 1928 Broadway hit *Holiday* had first been filmed in 1930 by Pathé, a subsidiary of RKO. The film was a success, and earned Academy Award nominations for leading lady Ann Harding, as well as for the script.

In the wake of the success of *The Awful Truth*, Columbia dusted off the story and decided *Holiday* would be the perfect vehicle to re-team Cary Grant and Irene Dunne. Unfortunately, given the strict period of time when Grant would be available to shoot the picture, Dunne would still be tied up over at RKO making *Joy of Living* (a 1938 film that Grant himself had passed on), thus necessitating another leading lady, a callous twist of fate that Dunne long regretted.

At this point, Katharine Hepburn inserted herself into the process. A decade earlier as a young and unknown stage actress, she had understudied Hope Williams, who starred in the original Broadway play as Linda Seton. Unfortunately for Hepburn, Miss Williams missed only one of her 229 shows, giving her understudy only the barest taste of the glory of playing the lead in the hit show. Hepburn loved the play and lamented that she never had the opportunity to make the part her own; she had partially consoled herself several years later by doing a scene from *Holiday* as her screen test for RKO[22]. Now however, learning that Columbia was making a new version, and that they were looking for the female lead, she reached out to Harry Cohn and asked for the part. The mogul

---

22 At the *Holiday* wrap party, Cukor surprised Hepburn by revealing that he had procured a copy of her screen test, which he then proceeded to play for the guests. Hepburn cringed at her over-earnest dramatics and large gestures in the clip. The rest of the partygoers got a good laugh from it, though.

liked the idea; *Stage Door* was still doing good business at the box office, and the advance buzz for the as-yet-unreleased *Bringing Up Baby* was that it was a likely hit, so quickly reteaming Hepburn and Grant seemed like a smart move. Columbia and RKO quickly worked out the details of borrowing the actress.

Next, Hepburn began campaigning for George Cukor to direct the film, a suggestion that Grant supported, as he well recalled the strong performance that the director had coaxed out of him in *Sylvia Scarlett*. Cohn was dubious he could get Cukor, as the director (then under contract to independent producer David O. Selznick) was known in Hollywood to be temperamentally rejecting every film offer being put to him at that time. With Hepburn's cajoling . . . she and Cukor were close friends, their relationship stretching back to her first film, 1932's *A Bill of Divorcement*, which he had directed . . . he acquiesced.

The remainder of the cast quickly began to fill. Constance Bennett was sought to play Linda's sister Julia, but she was already committed elsewhere, so Doris Nolan was chosen instead. One interesting bit of casting was Edward Everett Horton in the role of Professor Nick Potter . . . the very same role that Horton played in the original 1930 film. This was less any sort of nod to the first cinema version, and more a case of simply casting an accomplished character actor whom audiences recognized and liked.

Handling the scripting chores were veteran writers Sidney Buchman and Donald Ogden Stewart. The latter had a very direct connection to the original stage play. In the Twenties Stewart had been a Broadway playwright and was a good friend of Philip Barry. In fact, Barry had specifically written the part of Professor Potter for his friend to perform, although Stewart was not an actor. Nevertheless, he consented to do the role, and enjoyed himself tremendously on stage. Now, tasked with bringing the story to the screen, Stewart was determined to make this script a crowning achievement, as an act of thanks to Barry.

In the movie, Grant plays Johnny Case, who through years of hard work has elevated himself from a hardscrabble childhood to an adulthood of some success and modest comfort, with excellent prospects in business ahead of him. He meets Julia Seton while on vacation. He's bedazzled by her beauty and charm, and almost in spite of himself, he concludes that he's in love with her, as she says she is with him.

Julia brings Johnny home to meet her family. The Setons are wealth personified ... something which Case was not aware of in advance ... with Julia indulging in the role of heiress. The unconventional member of the family is Julia's sister, Linda (Hepburn's role). The third sibling is Ned, portrayed by Lew Ayers, whose spirit has been broken by relentless pressure from his father, and who has fled into alcohol and sarcasm to cope.

A prominent banker, Edward Seton is a stuffy snob, and initially he is unhappy with Julia's choice of Johnny, but he comes around and is much more welcoming after making some outside inquiries into Johnny's life and career. In fact, he insists that Johnny come work at the bank, which would be a respectable occupation for the man who marries his daughter. To the surprise of both Mr. Seton and Julia, Johnny declines the job.

As Johnny explains to Linda, with whom he's quickly bonded as something of a kindred spirit, "I've been working since I was ten. I want to find out *why* I'm working. It can't just be to pay bills and pile up more money. Even if you do, the government's going to take most of it." Linda asks him what the answer is, and he replies, "That's what I intend to find out. The world's changing out there. There are a lot of new, exciting ideas running around. Some may be right, and some may be cockeyed but they're affecting all our lives. I want to know how I stand, where I fit in the picture, what it's all gonna mean to me." His aim is to make enough money to hold him over while he takes a lengthy holiday. "I want to save part of my life for myself," he explains. "There's a catch to it, though. It's gotta be part of the young part. You know, retire young, work old, come back and work when I know what I'm working for."

Julia agrees to let Linda throw a small engagement party for her and Johnny on New Year's Eve, with just a few friends, but Mr. Seton decides that a larger, grander party is more suited for his daughter. Irked at being shunted aside, Linda spends the evening upstairs in the attic playroom, the place where she had such fun as a child with her mother before her passing. She's joined by Johnny's friends, Nick and Susan Potter (Edward Everett Horton and Jean Dixon), who got themselves lost exploring the Setons' vast Park Avenue mansion. Ned then arrives with servants bearing champagne. Linda sourly admits she's unhappy she was unable to give her party, and Ned comments about Johnny that "Julia's got his hair slicked down and Father's seeing that he meets the important people." Looking at the four of them, Prof. Potter proclaims, as if reading a newspaper society column, "Miss Linda Seton, on New Year's Eve, entertained a small group of Very Unimportant People."

Down in the party, Johnny finds Julia and tells her with equal parts incredulity and acerbity, "Believe it or not, I've just been learning how much it costs to keep up a yacht." But Julia is in a dither; Linda's absence is starting to prove embarrassing, so she dispatches Johnny to find her sister and make her come down to the party. Entering the playroom, he's mildly rebuked by the Potters for putting on airs for the Setons. Admonished and embarrassed, Case musses his own hair to prove that the "real" Johnny is still there. The delinquent quintet then have their own party upstairs, highlighted by Johnny and Linda doing acrobatics together (having learned to trust Grant's prowess making *Bringing Up Baby*, Hepburn by now was not only willing to do some tumbling tricks of her own with him, but she was practically insisting on it).

Linda has fallen in love with Johnny, but out of respect for her sister, she'll keep it a secret shared only with Ned. But Julia is mad at Johnny because he refused her father's job offer, and she dismisses his goals as silly talk. Left alone together as midnight nears, Johnny and Linda dance to the sound of a music box as his confidence cracks and he admits doubts in himself. At the stroke of twelve, they nearly kiss, but Linda then pulls away and tells him to return to Julia.

Johnny hopes to patch things up by inviting Julia to join him and the Potters on a trip to Europe, but she declines. Johnny then submits, compromising his own core beliefs by telling the Setons he'll agree to work at the bank for two years. Satisfied, Mr. Seton then takes charge of their wedding and honeymoon, plotting it out like a business transaction (and indeed, it will be as much business as pleasure for Johnny as he carries out bank obligations on their trip).

Realizing he's made a dreadful mistake, Johnny begs Julia to elope with him that very night, and then sail away to Europe. She rejects this, and Johnny understands at last that she is not the woman he could love. He leaves to join the Potters aboard ship.

Linda has finally had enough, angrily confronting her family, and then leaves the Setons far behind her as she storms out of the house. She rushes down to the docks and boards the liner to find Johnny, who spots her amid a flip he's doing, causing him to belly flop to the floor in surprise. And they kiss at last.

●●●

Holiday was no screwball comedy, but rather a comedy of manners. The humor was scripted to be barbed, rather than wacky. Stewart and Buchman retained much of Barry's original story and dialogue, but modernized it in places, and added some wit of their own. For Grant, it was a stark departure from his previous work, in particular the trio of wild comedies he had most recently made. He underplays his Johnny Case, replacing his usual charm with an eager earnestness. If George Kerby and Jerry Warriner had been the smartest guys in the room (or at least thought they were), Johnny Case knows he's bright, but also accepts that he has a lot to learn.

George Cukor was uninterested in having the polished, glib Cary Grant in this film, and he helped break the actor down to find this performance. When we meet Johnny, he looks like a man who wants to *be* Cary Grant, but isn't quite getting it; his clothes, while not ill-fitting, lack the tailored cut of Grant's usual attire[23]. His bowtie seems out of place. His hair is tousled, rather than smoothly combed and parted. His shoulders slouch, and his eyes dart around as he tries to take everything in, like a small town tourist in the big city for the first time. But he's no fool, appearances and philosophies aside.

Some bits of political commentary are injected into the film. Mr. Seton is indignant, and perhaps even a little afraid, of Johnny's intent to take his holiday from work, labeling his attitude "un-American", when what he doubtless means to say is communistic.

---
23 Doubtless this was one instance where the studio provided the wardrobe, rather than Grant.

And when a haughty couple from the party, the Crams (Linda dubs them "the witch and Dopey"), with their talk of wealth and how the country doesn't have the "right kind of government", come up to the attic, the playroom revelers intuitively greet them with stiff-armed Nazi salutes.

❋❋❋

The 1930s were a time when the cinema definition of 'sophisticated comedy' could encompass everything from screwball lunacy to Marx Brother anarchy to Noel Coward's drawing room farces, and moviegoers often turned out in large numbers for it all. So, Columbia had no fear that audiences might be confused by this shift in tone from what they had come to expect from a Cary Grant comedy.

To not mislead anyone into thinking this was simply a re-release of the 1930 film, Columbia briefly considered retitling their new version as *Unconventional Linda*. Thankfully, that idea was quickly abandoned. But unconventional would be the word for a marketing tactic launched by the studio, which instead of ignoring Hepburn's label as box office poison, instead embraced it, at least to refute it. IS IT TRUE WHAT THEY SAY ABOUT HEPBURN? the studio's public relations men fed to gossip columnists, certain that the success of the film would redeem the actress.

Opening on June 15th, the film was met with largely positive reviews. *Newsweek* dubbed it "brilliant" and praised Hepburn's performance, although *The New Republic* struck a sour note, complaining the film was "mechanical and shrill". Columnist Ed Sullivan of the *New York Daily News* raved about it, saying "Is it true what they say about Hepburn? If they say she is one of the three greatest American movie actresses, it's true what they say about Hepburn. With her back to the wall, [Hepburn] delivers one of the finest performances of her career." Columbia was so appreciative of his review, they ran it as an advertisement in the movie trade magazines. By and large, virtually all the critics' reviews…even the ones that didn't much care for the film…complimented Grant on his performance.

In its initial run in big city movie palaces, *Holiday* did very well, and looked to be a profitable hit, but then it moved on to the smaller towns outside of the metropolitan areas, and here it failed to find an audience. The Hollywood buzz on the film went from "hit" to "flop," although ultimately it did effectively break even at the box office. Following as it did the money-losing *Bringing Up Baby*, the widespread conclusion was that Katharine Hepburn was indeed box office poison.

Now free of her RKO contract, and with no other immediate Hollywood prospects (she hoped to be cast as Scarlett O'Hara in David O. Selznick's *Gone with the Wind* (1939), which Cukor was set to direct, but Selznick considered her all wrong for the part), Hepburn left Hollywood behind and returned to the East Coast, where she intended to resume her Broadway career. It looked to virtually everyone that she had retreated in defeat, but in fact it was a strategic withdrawal. Hollywood had not heard the last of her.

While *Bringing Up Baby* and *Holiday* were both considered by the public at large to be flops, the blame for their failings seemed to rest solely on Hepburn's shoulders, and no one impugned Grant. Continuing to ride high on the tremendous success of *The Awful Truth*, he was still considered to be a rising star. But he knew his luck in this regard could not hold out much longer. One more under-performing film, no matter how much the critics liked it, and Grant knew full well that his star would rapidly start to descend. It all rested on what RKO could find for him to do next.

● ● ●

Too anxious to wait too long between films, Grant was happy that filming on his next picture would begin just days after *Holiday*'s June premiere. In the meantime, he took a two-week vacation in Waikiki, Hawaii…without Phyllis Brooks. Things with "Brooksie" had been going very well over the past year, and the gossip columns were full of predictions of their inevitable wedding. True to form, Grant had begun touching on the subject of marriage with her but declined as yet to fully commit to a proposal, much less an actual wedding date. The Hawaiian excursion was a chance to put some distance between them so that he could more soberly examine their relationship. She let him go without protest in the hopes that he would finally get off the fence and put a ring on her finger.

●●●

Later that year, in October, Grant took the Super Chief to New York City, then sailed for England (again, without Brooks). It would be his first visit back to the UK since he had filed to become the legal guardian of his mother and arranged for Elsie Leach to be released from the sanitarium, setting her up with her own home in Bristol. He had wanted her to move to Southern California, but she considered the very idea preposterous. Elsie wanted to be near her family and friends, in the place she knew.

To date, their relationship had had plenty of complexities. Cary tried to write dutifully, but his mother still often complained it wasn't enough; eventually he established a routine where he would either send her a telegram or else call her via transatlantic phone on Sunday evenings, even if he was on location. Their letters to one another could be effusive in their declarations of love and affection, and with ample bits of playfulness, but in person their meetings were awkward and uneasy, with Cary frequently at a loss for words, and Elsie often tetchy. Beyond the home and the allowance which he provided, Elsie was uninterested in any of the lavish gifts her son bestowed on her. When he presented her with a mink coat, she dismissed it as unnecessary, since she already had a perfectly good wool coat, and she handed the fur back to him. She would give away the flowers he brought her. To others she would speak very fondly of him, but rarely as her son, rather instead as just someone she knew. For quite a long time, she would address him as Cary, and not Archie. It was as if she had lost both of her sons, not just her first, and her mind was unwilling to accept that Archie still lived. Grant couldn't help but feel some sense of relief when the visit finally concluded, and he sailed back to America. Nevertheless, he promised Elsie he would return the following summer.

●●●

On the trip back, Grant was able to put Archie Leach behind him once again, and he got to play the role of Cary Grant to the hilt, swapping stories and singing vaudeville songs with fellow passengers Marlene Dietrich, Gracie Fields, and studio mogul Jack Warner. Phyllis Brooks was awaiting him when the ship docked, and they spent the next several days painting the town red and enjoying Manhattan in the holiday season. Their festivities were dampened however when both were served subpoenas.

A huckster named William P. Buchner, Jr., who among other things claimed to be the fiancé of actress Loretta Young, had approached various celebrities in Hollywood . . . not only Grant and Brooks, but also Ronald Colman, Miriam Hopkins, Bing Crosby and United Artists Chairman Joseph Schenck, among other notable names . . . and asked them to buy into a plan to artificially manipulate the bond value of the Philippine Railway. Among Buchner's confederates was a prominent member of the Philippine National Assembly, Felipe Buencamino (the son of a leader of the Filipino revolution against Spain), who leaked false reports indicating that the Commonwealth government was about to take control of the railway, which caused the value of the bonds to skyrocket, at which point Buchner and his partners sold their bonds and pocketed the huge profits. Then the Commonwealth announced there was no plan for the government to take over the railroad, causing the bonds to crash, and costing the hoodwinked celebrities their investments. The U.S. government brought charges against Buchner for mail fraud, and soon the entire scheme was unraveled. As Grant and Brooks had declined to participate in the plan when first approached, their involvement in the case ended almost as soon as it began, but simply having their names attached to the affair in the initial press coverage was embarrassing for Grant.

As an investor, Grant tended to be cautious when it came to stocks and bonds, rarely taking real risks. Where he was bold was in money trading, and he read the financial pages thoroughly each day, frequently calling his broker to instruct him to buy or sell pounds sterling, francs, lira, yen and many other global currencies.

By accounts, Grant was particularly adept at this, and earned tidy profits from his trading.

●●●

While the major studios were still steadfastly turning their gazes away from Grant, he nevertheless had no lack of film projects pitched to him. Columbia wanted to team him with Marlene Dietrich in what would be their first pairing since *Blonde Venus* in 1932 but hadn't yet come up with a script for them to consider (and in fact never would, and Grant and Dietrich never shared the screen again).

British film producer Herbert Wilcox had just come over to RKO along with his wife, actress Anne Neagle, and wanted Grant to co-star with her in a biopic of the famous English music hall singer and actress, Marie Lloyd. At first glance it might appear as an appealing project for Grant, given his love of the music hall. However, Lloyd's life was a tragic one, and the only conceivable roles for Grant as the male lead would either be as her cuckold husband, who is driven to drink until it kills him, or else her lover, a horse jockey (which would have been ridiculous for the 6'2" Grant to try to carry off) who was an alcoholic who savagely beat Lloyd. The sordid details of Lloyd's life were well known and still widely remembered nearly twenty years after her death, and no amount of Hollywood gloss could put a happier luster on her story. The best that could be done, Grant reckoned, would be to write an entirely new story about a fictional woman. He passed on the film, and it was never made.

Universal approached Grant with a project that was, if possible, even more impractical than the Marie Lloyd film: an American adaptation of Jean Renoir's 1931 French film *La Chienne*. Grant instantly knew that this brutal story of a prostitute, her violent pimp, and the meek clerk who befriends her, is betrayed, and then murders her, would never pass the censors. Not even the title (translating into English as *The Bitch*) could be used. He wished Universal good luck with this one and turned it down[24].

24 Universal did not give up on the project, and in 1945 produced a much watered-down version of the story under the title *Scarlet Street*, starring Edward G. Robinson.

1938 would prove to be to that date the highest grossing year in Hollywood's history, and 1939 promised to do even better. It galled Grant that his two releases in that year didn't contribute much to the industry's overall box office, but he was confident that would change in the year to come. For Columbia, he would be working again with Howard Hawks, this time on a dramatic film.

However, first would come the picture he just wrapped up after months of location work in the Sierra Nevada range, a film that Grant could feel down to his very bones would be a huge hit.

New to Hollywood, new to films, and Paramount's newly-minted leading man. Even his name, Cary Grant, was brand new.

After five years as a contract player, he had achieved success and fame, but he did not see his stardom growing, or even sustaining, if he remained in the studio system. He would shock that system by striking out on his own as a freelance actor.

The first producer to take advantage of Grant's independent status was Hal Roach, himself something of a Hollywood maverick. Roach was gambling the future of his small studio on the success of this film.

Like many Hollywood actors, Grant earned extra money providing his name for advertising, in this instance cigarettes. He would later give up smoking, and strongly encourage his friends to quit the habit as well.

While TOPPER *was a great success, it was his next film that would be a smash hit, and which would firmly establish the on-screen persona that would make him a household name for decades to come. Take note in this ad that Columbia is encouraging filmgoers who had already seen Frank Capra's* LOST HORIZON *once to see it again, as the studio desperately tried to turn a profit on the budget-busting epic. It was Capra's costly overruns making this film that prompted Columbia head Harry Cohn to put Grant and director Leo McCarey together for* THE AWFUL TRUTH.

Leo McCarey's erratic and unpredictable filmmaking techniques caused plenty of headaches for Harry Cohn and drove Grant to beg to be let loose from the film, with the actor even offering $5000 to Columbia to release him. But there proved to be a method to McCarey's madness, and the finished film earned critical acclaim and was a huge box office success. Grant would never doubt McCarey's talents again.

Columbia's advertising campaign for the film included this faux magazine article.

Grant and Irene Dunne connected on-screen in a way few movie couples do, displaying a shared sparkling wit and encouraging one another to improvise during their scenes.

Katharine Hepburn, RKO's biggest star, saw her career in trouble following a string of box office flops. The studio hoped that putting her in a comedy alongside Grant would restore her fortunes. Director Howard Hawks set out to make the screwiest of screwball comedies, and both Hepburn and Grant displayed brilliant comedic skills together.

RKO was unhappy about Grant's decision to wear glasses for this role, as part of his effort to evoke the image of silent film star Harold Lloyd, on whom he patterned his performance. In the film's advertising, the studio dispensed with the spectacles as often as possible.

Immediately after BRINGING UP BABY, *Grant and Hepburn teamed again, this time at Columbia for* HOLIDAY. *Like ...BABY, this film underperformed in theaters, despite critical plaudits for the performances of the two lead actors. For Grant, failure to follow up the financial success of* THE AWFUL TRUTH *in his next two outings threatened to derail his career as an independent. He could be forgiven for starting to wonder if he had made a mistake leaving Paramount to strike out on his own.*

But any worries that his career was in jeopardy were thoroughly erased by GUNGA DIN, which proved to be one of the biggest hits of 1939, and a major release in what film aficionados now look upon as Hollywood's Golden Year.

GUNGA DIN *was equal parts Rudyard Kipling along with* THE THREE MUSKETEERS *by Alexandre Dumas. Grant stole the film by not only playing the comic role…a part he in fact was not originally cast for…but also displaying the athletic prowess he learned in his youth as a professional tumbler.*

After a string of comedies, Grant surprised fans by next choosing a dramatic role. The direction of Howard Hawks brought out a dark intensity in Grant's performance that proved he had at last become more than just a good-looking leading man; he was an excellent dramatic actor as well.

Originally called THE KIND MEN MARRY, *RKO changed the title to* IN NAME ONLY *at the last minute, but not before the first round of advance publicity had gone out to exhibitors. A soapy melodrama in which Carole Lombard was the real star, this was a curious film choice for Grant to make at that stage in his career.*

For Grant, most likely the best thing about making this "women's weeper" was working with Lombard, a longtime friend from their days together at Paramount. The actress had followed Grant's lead and become a freelancer, and in 1939 was the highest-paid actress in the United States.

From shortly after his arrival in Hollywood and throughout the 1930s, Grant's best friend was fellow actor Randolph Scott. Their co-habitation together in a luxurious beach house, publicly spotlighted by often ill-considered magazine photo spreads engineered by Paramount, fueled rumors of a romantic relationship between them.

Following his brief marriage to actress Virginia Cherrill, Grant dated a number of women, but the one he got most serious about was Phyllis Brooks. They discussed marriage, and he often told friends he was anxious to start a family with "Brooksie," but time and again he was unwilling to fully commit and set a date to be wed.

Grant and Irene Dunne made for one of the most successful screen couples of their day. The three films they made together earned millions at the box office.

Howard Hawks could be a difficult director for some actors to deal with, but Grant understood him and his idiosyncrasies as well as anyone, and helped co-star Rosalind Russell also successfully grasp his methods, resulting in electrifying performances from each of them.

Hawks encouraged Grant, Russell, and Ralph Bellamy to put their own spins on the script, resulting in improvised moments that added to the brilliant lunacy of HIS GIRL FRIDAY.

What was supposed to be the triumphant reteaming of Grant, Dunne and director Leo McCarey began with the tragedy of McCarey's near-fatal automobile accident, which hospitalized him and kept him from directly overseeing the day-to-day filming on the set. He continued to produce the movie from afar, but his absence deprived the film of his off-the-cuff inspirations, and it showed on the screen. The result was a good comedy, but not a great one on a par with THE AWFUL TRUTH.

By this point in his career, Grant could have demanded top billing. But out of deference to their friendship as well as his respect for her talents, he had Dunne's name listed first in the credits.

Another unusual career move for Grant. He was uncertain that he was a good fit for an historical costume drama, and his instincts proved correct. Still, he feared he couldn't keep making screwball comedies and romantic melodramas forever, so he wanted to try and establish himself in a different film genre. Unfortunately, this effort didn't work.

Realizing that THE HOWARDS OF VIRGINIA *might have a hard time finding its audience, Columbia sought to lure female filmgoers by widely sharing this promotional photo of Grant bathing, hoping the sex appeal would sell tickets.*

When he embarked on his freelance career in 1937, Grant found himself unwanted by most of Hollywood's major studios. But by 1940 his stardom and audience appeal were undeniable, so MGM...the biggest major of them all...finally cast him in what proved to be one of the biggest hit films of the year.

Grant often passed the time between takes on the set banging away at a piano, frequently singing the old showtunes that he lovingly learned as a teenager performing as a tumbler in English music halls.

After three years independently guiding his own career, Cary Grant had emerged as one of Hollywood's biggest stars, and had laid the foundation for his immortality as an icon.

1939

By the livin' Gawd that made you: *Gunga Din*

The idea of bringing Rudyard Kipling's 1890 poem "Gunga Din" to the screen had been around Hollywood very nearly as long as there had been a Hollywood. The problem was that no one had yet figured out how to translate the story of the gallant but much-maligned Hindu water bearer into a cohesive film.

The poem proved particularly enduring, even long after the glittering grandeur of Queen Victoria's British Raj had given way to a desultory occupation of a sub-continent that was growing increasingly restless at being governed from afar by London. Kipling's key line, "You're a better man than I am, Gunga Din," still found itself in common conversational usage.

In 1936 RKO had acquired the screen rights to the poem from producer Edward Small and assigned novelist William Faulkner to work on a script. It's unclear who came up with the idea of merging "Gunga Din" with another Kipling work, his *Soldiers Three* (1888) collection of short stories . . . it may well have been Faulkner . . . but this was at last the breakthrough that allowed a film story to be structured around the basic elements of the poem.

Faulkner only worked on the script for a month or so before it was temporarily shelved. In 1937 it was dusted off and offered to Howard Hawks as the first production of his new multi-film deal with the studio. He turned to screenwriters Ben Hecht and Charles MacArthur to work up a screenplay. They decided to borrow liberally from one of their own earlier hits, *The Front Page* (1931), which had been a successful stage play and then an equally successful motion picture. In *The Front Page*, reporter Hildy Johnson announces he's quitting his newspaper and getting married, while his editor, Walter Burns, connives to keep his star newsman by hook or by crook. In the end, Burns seems to acquiesce to the inevitable, even gifting his own pocket watch to Hildy as a farewell gift. After Johnson and his fiancée leave to catch their train, Burns calls his assistant and orders him to wire the chief of police in the first town the train stops in with a full description of Hildy with orders to arrest him, because "the son of a bitch just stole my watch!"

In their treatment for *Gunga Din* (1939), Sgt. Ballantine informs his two friends, MacChesney and Cutter (the names changed from Kipling's original characters, Leyroyd, Mulvaney and Ortheris), that he is resigning from Her Majesty's Army to marry his sweetheart and go work for her father in his tea business. MacChesney and Cutter scheme to convince Ballantine to stay in the service. Cutter eventually finds himself caught in a life-or-death situation and in need of rescuing. Ballantine is ready to spring to his aid, but his resignation is about to go into effect, precluding him from joining the troop on its relief mission. MacChesney says if Ballantine re-ups his enlistment, then once Cutter is safe and sound, Mac will tear it up, and Ballantine will be free to leave with his fiancée. Ballantine unhesitatingly signs the paper, and the troops rescue Cutter, with Gunga Din, the regiments' native water bearer, heroically giving his life to save the three sergeants. Ballantine then departs for civilian life, and MacChesney . . . who in fact has not destroyed the reenlistment paperwork, but instead has passed it up to his commander . . . orders the Sergeant-at-Arms to arrest Ballantine for desertion.

Other than some exterior action scenes, much of Hecht and MacArthur's script is interior bound, and given the obvious tilt toward humor, RKO was considering it as a vehicle for comedic actor Jack Oakie. However, because Hecht was also writing the screenplay for *Nothing Sacred* (1937), while MacArthur was likewise occupied with *Angels with Dirty Faces* (1938), and both were contributing uncredited work to various other scripts, as well as collaborating on a new play, *Ladies and Gentlemen* (1939), their work on *Gunga Din* went slowly. RKO also wasn't happy with some of what they were writing, feeling the stance their script conveyed was a bit too pro-Indian, rather than playing up the Imperial splendor of the British (as author and screenwriter Donald Ogden Stewart once said when asked to describe his two friends, "they were always for the underdog."). At one point the studio sent some pages back to the writers with a note attached that read, "You just don't seem to understand the white man's burden." Hecht and MacArthur fired back, "The white man's burden seems to be making lots of money. Since we're both white, how about an advance of $20,000?"

At the pace the writers were going, it looked likely they wouldn't be able to turn in a completed script until much later than RKO wanted. Finally, Hecht and MacArthur left the production altogether, and Hawks brought in Dudley Nichols, who among many other accomplishments had written a screen adaptation of Alexandre Dumas's *The Three Musketeers* (1935), and he and Hawks now sought to inject some of that literary classic's swashbuckling "One for All and All for One" camaraderie into *Gunga Din*. Pulling together a coherent script (which at that point was still using Hecht and MacArthur's *The Front Page* as the foundation of its story) was proving more laborious than expected, and it looked as if there would not be a completed shooting script ready until later in 1938. Not wanting to keep Hawks idle all that time, the studio put him and Nichols on *Bringing Up Baby* (1938) in the meantime.

When *Bringing Up Baby* failed to perform at the box office as expected, and Hawks was subsequently let go by the studio, RKO assigned George Stevens to direct *Gunga Din*. He did not seem to be an obvious choice, in that his past work was rooted in several of Katharine Hepburn's romantic dramas, a couple of Fred Astaire and Ginger Rogers musicals, and a few of Bert Wheeler and Robert Woolsey's double entendre-laden comedies, and not the outdoor adventure that RKO was now starting to envision *Gunga Din* to be.

Historical fiction films set in 19th Century India and featuring heroic British soldiers had become popular and profitable in Hollywood in recent years, with such box office successes as *Lives of a Bengal Lancer* (1935), *Clive of India* (1935), *The Charge of the Light Brigade* (1936), and even *Wee Willie Winkle* (1937) with Shirley Temple. Cary Grant (sporting a Clark Gable-ish moustache) even spent some time in the (relative) vicinity in *The Last Outpost* (1935), set in Kurdistan during the Great War.

Stevens was highly enthusiastic about the film and urged RKO to think even bigger than it had been. He saw *Gunga Din* as a sprawling comedic adventure, chock full of the spirits of not only of the Musketeers, but also cowboy and gangster movies, the *Terry and the Pirates* newspaper strip, *Boys' Own Magazine*, and the *Thrilling Adventures* pulps.

RKO appointed Joel Sayre and Fred Guiol to write the screenplay, incorporating as much of the earlier versions into their work as they could[25]. Sayre, a novelist, had screenwriting experience with such films as *Come On, Marines!* (1934) and *Annie Oakley* (1935), which combined drama with adventure, while Guiol first learned his trade working for Hal Roach's comedies in the Twenties, writing and directing shorts with Laurel & Hardy (George Stevens had also worked with Laurel & Hardy for Roach).

As the new script took form, studio production head Pandro S. Berman and the RKO executives back in New York debated the budget they should assign. Stevens was pushing for this to be the highest quality 'A' picture the studio could produce. In a coming year that was already promising landmark motion pictures… MGM's *Wizard of Oz*; Samuel L. Goldwyn's *Wuthering Heights*; Columbia's *Mr. Smith Goes to Washington*; and of course, David O. Selznick's *Gone with the Wind*…Stevens advocated for *Gunga Din* to be RKO's bid for greatness in the Class of '39. His argument carried the day, and the production was awarded a budget of $1,300,000, more money than RKO had ever committed to a film before.

Casting the film came next. There was no question that Cary Grant would play the lead role of Ballantine, and he readily agreed. Next, RKO borrowed Victor McLaglen from Twentieth Century-Fox for the part of MacChesney. Amusingly, although a Brit of Scottish heritage, McLaglen instead found himself Hollywood's go-to actor for Irish roles in the wake of his Academy Award as Best Actor in *The Informer* (1935), and appropriately he would play one here as well.

---

25 The film's final credits would read: screenplay by Sayre and Guiol, from a story by Hecht and MacArthur, from Kipling's poem.

For a time, Jack Oakie was still considered for the role of Cutter. But Berman had been looking for a vehicle for Douglas Fairbanks, Jr. that would be a hit. His two most recent films for RKO (after Grant, he too had signed a non-exclusive contract with the studio), *Joy of Living* (1938) and *Having Wonderful Time* (1938), both comedies, had fizzled at the box office. But a rousing adventure film he had made for Selznick, *The Prisoner of Zenda* (1937), had been a huge hit. Berman hoped that adding Fairbanks to the cast would bolster the actor's stock for further RKO films to follow. And so, he became Cutter (but only after a story erroneously emerged in the press that George Sanders would be cast instead.)

For the title role of Gunga Din himself, Berman wanted to cast a 14-year-old Indian actor named Selar Sabu[26] (known professionally only as Sabu), who had recently made his film debut in another Kipling adaptation, *Elephant Boy* (1937), for British producer Alexander Korda. Unfortunately for RKO, Sabu wasn't available, as Korda was featuring him in yet another film based on a Kipling work, *The Jungle Book* (1940).

Garson Kanin, a Broadway actor, director and playwright who had recently come to Hollywood to direct films, encouraged a friend, Sam Jaffe, to audition for the role. Unlike the young Sabu who was a native born Indian, Jaffe was a 47-year-old Russian Jewish immigrant from New York's Lower East Side – but he had just played the part of the High Lama in Frank Capra's *Lost Horizon* (1937) to excellent reviews, and he was confident he could pull off the role of Din as well. For his tryout, he recited Kipling's poem in full, having committed it to memory thirty years earlier as part of his (failed) audition to win a place in a school dramatics club. This time, his recitation succeeded, and he won the part of the water bearer.

Other prominent roles in the cast ... Abner Biberman as the villainous Chota, Joan Fontaine as Ballantine's fiancée, Emmy Stebbins, Robert Coote as Sgt. Higginbotham ... were quickly filled, and production was launched on June 24th, 1938 (without as yet a finished script). Sayre and Guiol had taken much of the film out of the indoor barracks where Hecht and MacArthur had placed it

---

26 Or Sabu Dastigar in some biographies.

and set the action in the rugged lands of Northwest India and the Khyber Pass, which was simulated in California's Sierra Nevada and Alabama Hills. This necessitated filming through the hottest days of summer, when the afternoon temperature would often top 100 degrees and more.

A veritable small town was built by RKO just outside of Lone Pine, California, featuring not only the sets for the film, but also quarters for six hundred cast and crew members, and stables for more than 250 horses and mules, along with four elephants.

Grant arrived deeply tanned from his recent Hawaiian vacation and looking as bronzed as a British soldier in India ought to be. The location shoot promised to be arduous, and it was. The unit worked seven days a week, almost always in extreme heat. Frequent delays were caused by dust storms as well as the occasional and unpredictable burst of rain. The animals could be temperamental, and so from time to time could some actors. Grant loved it all. He was having the time of his life.

Except filming had not proceeded without a very major shake-up. Just as the production was getting underway, Grant approached Fairbanks with a startling request: would he mind terribly if the two of them traded parts?

The more he had thought about it, the more Grant came around to the idea that Cutter was the better role for him. Fairbanks reminded him that Ballantine was the larger part, and that he got the girl in the end, but Grant insisted that he didn't mind that at all. Of course, Grant didn't have to say, nor did Fairbanks need to be told, that as the film's leading star, any role Grant played would out of necessity be expanded to fit his stature. As for not getting the girl…well, there are worse things than losing a lady to Douglas Fairbanks, Jr.

Fairbanks agreed to the switch, and they both approached Stevens, who was amiable to the change. He cleared it with Berman[27], and then Sayre and Guiol quickly went to work on the script, beefing up the part of Cutter (including, at Grant's request, giving him a

---

27 RKO's Publicity Department took advantage of the situation by telling reporters that Grant and Fairbanks, at the suggestion of Stevens, flipped a coin to see who would play which role. It's a nifty bit of Hollywood hokum, and one which both Grant and Fairbanks themselves enjoyed passing off as a "fact" years later.

first name: Archie) and looking for new opportunities to showcase Grant's acrobatics (which by now had become somewhat expected of him in his films). They also worked on Ballantine, scripting him to be more of an homage to Doug, Jr's legendary father, Douglas Fairbanks, Sr., who packed movie houses around the world in the 1920s with such exhilarating adventure films as *The Mark of Zorro* (1920), *The Three Musketeers* (1921) and *The Thief of Bagdad* (1924).

That change made, filming proceeded apace. Grant would wake each morning in the bungalow house that RKO had rented for him in Lone Pine and scour the financial pages of the Los Angeles newspaper he had specially delivered, then call or cable his brokers as to which currencies they should buy or sell that day. He then went to make up[28] and wardrobe, and was promptly on the set and ready to work when Stevens called "action". Despite the long hours and grueling weather, he found it all exhilarating. The entire experience had become something of a holiday camp for Grant, Fairbanks and McLaglen, who horsed around between takes like kids, often hazing one another with practical jokes.

However, it wasn't all fun and games with the lads for Grant, such as when he would invite Phyllis Brooks to come up to the location and spend weekends with him. Their see-saw relationship . . . he would go from ardently professing his love and telling her he wanted them to marry and have a big family together, and then the next day he would be detached and impassive with her . . . left her confused and dejected when they weren't together. She still loved him, but she was starting to suspect they just weren't working out.

In the film, following an opening scene that sets the stage for the adventure to come, we are introduced to Sergeants Cutter, Ballantine and MacChesney in what we can easily assume is a natural environment for them, a deck-clearing brawl with some Highland troops. When Cutter is called out by Sgt. Higginbotham, he is holding his opponent out of a second story window. When told to "take your hands off that man," Cutter obediently does as he is instructed...and, letting his man tumble to the ground below, he

---

28 Thanks to his deep tan, Grant needed far less make-up than most of the other actors, in particular Sam Jaffe, who daily endured several hours of having bronzer applied and then removed from nearly his entire body.

shrugs his shoulders as if to say, "Well, *you* told me to let him go." One suspects this funny bit of business came from Fred Guiol, as it seemed right out of the Hal Roach playbook. George Stevens was always on the lookout for clever bits of comedy to pepper the film with; and encouraged Grant in particular, to improvise.

    Back in Hollywood, Pandro Berman was viewing the rushes being shipped from Lone Pine with growing dismay. He had expected a rousing adventure film with romance and plenty of action. He had not expected Stevens to lean so heavily into humor, to the point where *Gunga Din* was seeming more like a satire of the very kind of film RKO was spending a rajah's ransom to make. Add to it, that the romance between Ballantine and Emmy was treated like an uninvited intrusion into the boys' club and was getting as minimal screen time as possible from the director (although her lack of screen time didn't deter 20-year-old actress Joan Fontaine from developing an unrequited crush on 33-year-old George Stevens).

    RKO would release 49 feature length films in 1939, plus multiple shorts and Pathé newsreels, in addition to distributing Walt Disney's cartoons, so the studio mogul had much more than *Gunga Din* and its worries to keep him busy. Berman briefly considered shutting the production down, and possibly firing Stevens from the film, but the delays would have added considerable cost to what was already a monumental investment from the studio, and also would have disrupted other production schedules (for instance, some of the cast and crew were slated to begin work on other movies once *Gunga Din* wrapped up filming, so any delay on that film would have had a costly domino effect on others). The RKO head finally concluded they had passed the point of no return; they had to push on and finish the film. He did urge Stevens to punch up the action, and the director and his actors responded with some battle scenes that Berman had to admit were rather pulse-pounding to watch, which pleased him.

    As the story quickly progresses, the Sergeants uncover that the Thuggee murder cult has been resurrected, and they are ordered to take a unit of soldiers to an outpost town taken by the Thuggees and take it back. Ballantine is reluctant to go, because his enlistment is about to end and he intends to marry his fiancée and work for her father, while MacChesney and Cutter try to figure out how to keep their friend in the army (which was taken straight from Hecht and MacArthur's original story). Meanwhile, Cutter has also been searching for a legendary cache of gold supposedly hidden in the region generations before, convinced that if he finds it, he'll live like an emperor for the rest of his life[29]. Gunga Din, the unit's loyal Bhishti water carrier, who desperately wants to be a British soldier himself, informs Cutter that he has discovered the temple of gold not far away. Excited, Cutter tells MacChesney he's going to find the gold, but MacChesney thinks he's on a fool's errand, and at any rate, Cutter is needed on the mission to hold the town and reestablish telegraph communications with their regimental headquarters. MacChesney orders Cutter imprisoned for attempted desertion and has him locked in a cell until he can get over his obsession with the rumored gold.

That night, Cutter is able to escape with the help of Din, who brings an elephant to pull down a wall of the jail cell. Annie was a thirty-year-old pachyderm who had gotten her start in films in the early silent era, working for Thomas Edison's motion picture company. She made $450 a week and rated her own stand-in so that she didn't have to loiter in the hot sun while camera shots were blocked out. At one point before the final shooting script had been assembled, there had been discussion of having the film conclude with a massive elephant charge to rout the Thuggees. That idea lasted only until someone in the studio's accounting department calculated how much it would cost to rent, transport and tend the requisite number of elephants from circuses and private zoos across the country to the set.

The pair go to the hidden temple, and it is indeed laden with a fortune in gold, diamonds, and other gems – but it is also the secret fortress of the Thuggees, and Cutter and Din overhear Guru, the Kali cult leader, commanding his devotees, "Rise and kill. Kill, lest you be killed yourself. Kill for the love of killing. Kill for the love of Kali. Kill!" Cutter realizes the hundreds of Thuggees will over-

---

29 Just as the screenwriters liberally mined Alexandre Dumas's *The Three Musketeers* for this film, with this subplot they touched on another Dumas tale, *The Count of Monte Cristo* (1846).

whelm and massacre the British force, and then go on a murder rampage that might spread throughout all of India. He tells Din to rush back to the outpost and warn MacChesney and Ballantine. In the meantime, Cutter knows he must distract the cultists so that Din can make his escape undetected.

Stepping out from his hiding place, Cutter loudly and with a swaggering self-assurance that borders on unbridled cockiness announces, "You're all under arrest, the whole bunch of you…Her Majesty's very touchy about having her subjects strangled." It's a ludicrous moment; one lone, unarmed British soldier standing up to hundreds of murderous cultists. He does it knowing the result will most assuredly be his torture and death, but he does not hesitate, and he buys Gunga Din the time he needs to get out.

Din reaches the outpost, and MacChesney, realizing that an attack by the entire unit of troops would only get Cutter killed, elects to go alone so that he can slip in and rescue him. Ballantine insists he'll go too, but his discharge papers (along with his fiancée) have just arrived, and he is now a civilian, so MacChesney refuses to take him along. However, after further arguing between the two, MacChesney offers a compromise: if Ballantine will sign reenlistment papers, then and there, he'll be reinstated to his rank, and he can help rescue Cutter. MacChesney promises that once that's taken care of, he'll tear up the papers and Ballantine can depart with Emmy. Ballantine suspects a trick, but he realizes it's the only way he can save Cutter's life, so he signs up again.

Unfortunately for MacChesney, Ballantine and Din, they are captured by the Thuggees as soon as they enter the temple, and are placed in a cell with Cutter, who had been tortured. Guru demands to know where their regiment is, so that the cultists can ambush them. MacChesney pretends cowardice and offers to tell him everything, but this is just a ruse so that the soldiers can seize Guru and keep his cultists at bay by holding their leader hostage.

They take Guru with them to the temple rooftop, a much more defensible position should any of the Thuggees try to attack, and from that vantage point they can hear the bagpipes of the approaching regiment. They can also see the hundreds of armed

Thuggees[30] in position to attack the British column in the narrow pass, which would be a blood-spattered shooting gallery that would wipe out the unsuspecting regiment, which is still too far away to hear any shouts of warning. Guru, realizing that his followers are too worried for his safety to attack the three sergeants and their water-bearer, commits suicide by hurling himself to his death in a pit full of poisonous vipers. Their human shield gone, the quartet are swarmed by Thuggees, with Cutter being shot and bayoneted, and Gunga Din also takes a bayonet in the back, while Ballantine and MacChesney are seized and gagged.

The British troops approach the trap that has been laid for them, while MacChesney and Ballantine can only look on with dread, unable to cry out a warning. The Thuggees assume that Cutter and Din are dead and leave them unattended, but in fact they're only wounded. Cutter watches as Din cautiously takes a bugle from a dead Thuggee killed in the brief rooftop melee and then, despite his wounds, precariously climbs up the side of the temple's tower to the top of its golden dome.

Mere moments before the cultists are about to open fire on the British, Gunga Din sounds the call of warning on the bugle, until he is cut down by a hail of bullets from Guru's followers. The regiment's infantry and cavalry swiftly assemble into battle formation and go on the attack, overwhelming the Thuggees and putting an end to their murderous cult.

The last act of the film is held in the dark of night, with MacChesney, Ballantine and Cutter (on a stretcher) at attention while their regimental Colonel eulogizes Gunga Din, and proclaims that for his heroism, he is posthumously appointed as a corporal in the British Army. An English reporter, Rudyard Kipling (played by Reginald Sheffield), who was present at the battle, has composed a poem in honor of Din's heroism and sacrifice. The Colonel reads aloud from the last stanza, culminating in the immortal line, "You're a better man than I am, Gunga Din!"

---

30 RKO had taken pains to try and hire as many Indian actors as possible for the hundreds of extras needed for the film, but there simply weren't that many East Indians available in Hollywood. So, the ranks of both the Thuggees and the various native inhabitants were filled out with Hispanics, Native Americans, Pacific Islanders, and anyone else who looked the part.

As Din's body is placed into the fires of the funeral pyre, this somber moment is given a Hollywood happy ending of sorts, as we see the superimposed image of Gunga Din in the Hereafter, now garbed in the dress whites of a British Army corporal. He snaps a smart salute to the audience and beams a proud smile, as the soundtrack swells to the tune of "Auld Lang Syne".

●●●

Despite the seven-days-a-week shooting schedule, filming on location dragged on, although once that was completed and the production moved for interior scenes at the RKO studio, the pace picked up rapidly. Still, Stevens was some five weeks over schedule and a half-a-million dollars over budget when he finally completed the production in September. Given the cost, RKO deemed it virtually impossible for *Gunga Din* to return any sort of profit.

Never was a studio happier to be wrong. Released on January 24, 1939, it was an instant hit with critics and audiences alike. In North America it earned back what it cost to make, and overseas profits added nearly a million dollars more to that take. However, due to the rather arcane accounting practices of Hollywood, *Gunga Din* was still officially declared to have lost money, at least during its first theatrical release (later reissues finally pushed the ledger from red to black).

The film was a big hit in Great Britain as well, coming as it did at a critical moment in that nation's history. After the war scare with Germany in 1938 and the rapid unraveling of Prime Minister Neville Chamberlain's appeasement policy toward Adolf Hitler, the national attitude among the British people was moving away from the pacifism that grew following the harrowing Great War, toward a growing acceptance that a military stand was quite likely necessary in the days to come. When in September of '38 Britain and France sacrificed Czechoslovakia to the Nazis in exchange for a German promise of peace, Winston Churchill thundered at Chamberlain, "You were given the choice between war and dishonour. You chose dishonour and will have war." For many Brits at that time, Churchill was seen as a bellicose relic of a violent Imperial past. And yet, just a few months later, he was being reevaluated as a wise prophet. It was at this moment that *Gunga Din* arrived in theaters. Steeped as it was in Victorian martial splendor, when it was said that the sun never set on the British Empire, it stirred something in the breasts of Englishmen.

It could not be said that the film was embraced everywhere. In India, rather than hailing a glorious British past, it was seen as a degrading reminder of a sordid history, and the Indian nationalist movement condemned and boycotted *Gunga Din*. The colonial office outright banned it from being shown in certain parts of India, for fear it would inflame radical anti-British passions.

Another source of criticism was perhaps unexpected but should not have been surprising. The family of Rudyard Kipling (the author having died in 1936) protested that the screenwriters had made a hash of his work, and that the movie was more Dumas than Kipling. They also resented the inclusion of a fictionalized version of Kipling himself in the film, so for prints in the British Commonwealth, the Kipling character was excised.

These criticisms aside, the film was more than enough of a success to allow RKO to stake a claim as a major contributor to the body of important films of 1939, which later generations would herald as 'Hollywood's Greatest Year'. For Grant the film was a personal triumph, reaffirming that he was an important . . . and bankable . . . leading man, and helping dim the film industry's memory of the comparative box office failures of *Bringing Up Baby* and *Holiday*.

❊❊❊

The remainder of Grant and Brooksie's Christmastime of 1938 visit in New York following the subpoena debacle went from bad to worse, as Phyllis contracted pneumonia, and on the train ride back to Los Angeles had a fever that spiked at a life-threatening 105 degrees, and she fell unconscious. Grant spent hours each day at her hospital bedside, until she had recovered enough to return home where her mother would care for her. But he saw very little of her during that lengthy convalescence, because Grant and Phyllis's mother, Daisy Steiller, did not get along. In fact, Mrs. Steiller openly disapproved of him, and he grew to despise her. A morally conservative woman, she thought it was shameful how Grant and her daughter were cavorting about in public (and spending many nights together at his beach house) and were not observing a more traditional courtship. The fact that Grant had yet failed to marry her daughter was another black mark against him in Daisy Steiller's book, and she rarely hesitated to advise Phyllis to break things off with him.

All this personal tumult came at a time when Grant was launching a new and somewhat surprising career undertaking. When he was under contract to Paramount, he rarely made radio appearances, as the major studios believed that people were less likely to pay to see stars in movies if they could hear them for free over the airwaves. Rare exceptions for Grant were appearances on *The Lux Radio Theatre*, which was hosted by Paramount's preeminent director, Cecil B. DeMille. Once he had gone freelance however, Grant began accepting more radio work, and found it quite enjoyable. In 1938 he returned to the *Lux* program along with Irene Dunne, for an adaptation of her earlier hit film, *Theodora Goes Wild* (1936). Unfortunately for Dunne, when *Lux* finally did an adaptation of *The Awful Truth* in 1939, she was unavailable, and Claudette Colbert was tapped to play the female lead alongside Grant, reprising his film role.

In 1938 the J. Walter Thompson advertising agency approached the National Broadcasting Company (NBC) about possible new programs that their client, Kellogg's, could sponsor. In fact, NBC was developing a new weekly series unlike anything that had appeared on network radio before. It was called *The Circle*, and its premise was that it would principally be a round table discussion of important issues of the day, but also include dramatic, comedic and musical segments. The hook was that it would be hosted by four major Hollywood stars: Ronald Colman, Carole Lombard, Groucho Marx and Cary Grant. They would be joined each week by other prominent celebrities.

Kellogg's was dubious, not at all certain that their product was the right fit for such a unique concept, but with few other opportunities available just then to buy airtime, the cereal maker finally signed on.

It would prove to be a costly investment, with the weekly salaries for the hosts and their guests topping some $35,000; Grant himself would be receiving $5,000 a week for his services, a not-inconsiderable sum for radio.

The conceit of the show was that the four stars were members of a club, with Colman as the president, Lombard its secretary, and Grant holding the position of "Beadle", which is a fairly obscure term for an officer in a church organization who keeps order, but it was perhaps more appropriate to call him the show's court jester. While Groucho (with his brother Chico along as well) handled the outright comedy, Grant seemed to play a variation of his screwball comedy characters, making wisecracks and indulging his music hall roots by singing Noel Coward's "Mad Dogs and Englishmen" and, memorably, setting the FCC broadcasting rules to music and singing them.

The Circle debuted on Sunday, January 15 at 10:00 PM to a large listenership but only fair reviews from critics. Unfortunately, that was the high watermark in terms of audience, and the program began a steady descent in the ratings that culminated with its cancellation after six months. Despite a parade of noteworthy guests, including actors Basil Rathbone and Boris Karloff, sportswriter Grantland Rice, and conductor José Iturbi, listeners remained baffled by the ever-shifting tones of the show, as it veered from serious discussion to clowning, and with the musical interludes mixing classical with contemporary numbers. It didn't help any that the "freewheeling discussions" were clearly scripted. It wasn't long before Grant, Colman and Lombard found reasons to skip showing up (their contracts allowed them to come and go as they pleased), thus robbing the program of much of the star luster that was one of its few draws for listeners. By that June Kellogg's informed NBC that it was pulling its sponsorship, and *The Circle* was quietly retired for good.

Happily for Grant, the show was so quickly forgotten by the public at large, no one recalled it as a failure on his part. Happier still, his work on the silver screen was succeeding much more than *The Circle* ever had.

No tomorrows... just today: *Only Angels Have Wings*

Even as Brooksie was being hospitalized, filming began on Cary Grant's next film for Columbia. As director Howard Hawks was trying to shoot the film in chronological order as much as possible, and Grant's character was not in the opening scenes, he was not needed on the set at first, allowing him to stay at Phyllis's bedside.

After having been spurned by RKO, Hawks had made his way back to Columbia, where he was that rare filmmaker who had a good and friendly relationship with Harry Cohn, and rarer still Hawks was one of the few directors whom Cohn would allow to work at his own pace... within reason. In later years, Hawks would tell the story that he happened to drop by Cohn's office, and the mogul asked if he had any ideas for a script. The laconic director casually mentioned that he just so happened to have come up with an idea that very morning and had written out a few pages about it (which he conveniently had with him) if Cohn wanted to take a look. The studio head read it, loved it, and told Hawks he had a deal.

It's a fun yarn, but almost certainly untrue. In fact, the basic concept for the film was likely supplied by Columbia to Hawks, probably because Hawks... who was a U.S. Army flight instructor during the First World War, and an avid sport pilot ever since... may have expressed interest in doing another 'airplane picture' (having had tremendous success with *The Air Circus* in 1928, *The Dawn Patrol* in 1930, and *Ceiling Zero* in 1936). The story scenario he was given, "Plane Number Four", was written by magazine writer Anne Wigton and sold to Columbia in January of 1938.

Hawks went to work on his own scenario, utilizing much of what was in Wigton's synopsis, yet also creating characters based in part on pilots he had met in Mexico while he was scouting location scenes for *Viva Villa!* (1934). As he and Jules Furthman began writing the script, they named the film *Plane from Barranca*, but soon enough it was retitled *Only Angels Have Wings* (1939).

From the very start this was designated as Grant's next film for Columbia. Ironically, because he was fulfilling his obligation to Columbia at this time, Grant was unable to star in a film being shot concurrently over at RKO...a film that by any measure would have been the perfect vehicle for Cary Grant. *Love Affair* (1939) was Leo McCarey's first production since *The Awful Truth* (1937), and he again cast Irene Dunne as the female lead. The male starring role in this romantic melodrama seemed tailor-made for Grant, and reteaming him with Dunne and McCarey would have been a publicity bonanza, but with him not available, the part was given to French actor Charles Boyer. Grant himself was disappointed that circumstances didn't allow him to do the film; visiting Dunne on the set one day, he openly expressed his wish that he was making the picture with her[31].

Joining Grant in *Only Angels Have Wings* would be Jean Arthur as Bonnie Lee, an American entertainer working her way through South America. Hawks had relative freedom to fill most of the other roles, but Harry Cohn was insistent that Arthur be in the film. She was Columbia's biggest female star at the time and a cornerstone of Frank Capra's stock company of players, and if, as expected, Capra bolted from Columbia once his contract was up later that year, Cohn wanted to keep Arthur happy by providing her with quality roles in hit films. Hawks was unhappy with her in the part, because he believed her sprightly and wholesome personality, along with her peppy acting style, were entirely wrong for the tone of the movie. His instincts were soon matched by those of Arthur herself, who to her everlasting frustration felt she couldn't get a proper handle on her character. More frustrating still for her was Howard Hawks himself. Arthur was used to directors like Capra, John Ford and Mitchell Leisen, men who would explain what they wanted from the actress, and often act out the scene themselves to demonstrate it, but that wasn't the Hawks style. Taciturn even in his most loquacious moments, Hawks would provide scant guidance in how to act. If he didn't like a performance, he would sim-

---

31   Grant would however get his own chance at the part in 1957 when he starred in the remake, renamed *An Affair to Remember*. Irene Dunne, long since retired from acting, was replaced by Deborah Kerr, but Leo McCarey returned to direct.

ply call for take after take until the offender figured out what they needed to do to make it right. Grant had learned how to read the director's silences, and they got along well. Arthur quickly developed an adversarial relationship with Hawks that bordered on outright hostility.

After Bonnie Lee and Geoff Carter (Grant's character), the most important role was that of Bat MacPherson, a pilot haunted by the fact that he had once bailed out of a crashing plane, but his mechanic didn't and had died. That tragedy left Bat ostracized amongst other pilots back in the States, so he comes to Barranca for the only flying job he can get. For this role Hawks was steadfast in casting Richard Barthelmess. Once a major star in both the silent era as well as the early sound years (he had headlined in Hawks' *Dawn Patrol* in 1930), Barthelmess had seen his career dwindle until by this point, he hadn't had a single film role since 1936. What's more, a bungled plastic surgery procedure had left permanent scars beneath his eyes, further inhibiting his appeal to the studios. Hawks liked and respected Barthelmess and recognized him as an uncommonly good actor[32]. And in his opinion, the scars were a perfect touch for MacPherson, an outward glimpse of his wounded soul.

For the important part of Judy, MacPherson's wife (and Geoff Carter's former lover), Hawks had intended to cast a newcomer whose career he was promoting, Dorothy Comingore (then working under the stage name Linda Winters). But Cohn asked . . . not demanded, simply requested . . . that Hawks consider another young starlet whom Columbia had under contract, Rita Hayworth[33]. Hawks dutifully shot screen tests with Hayworth performing with Barthelmess and Arthur. The director hadn't been overly impressed with the ingenue when he first met her, finding her beautiful to be sure, but much too demure for what her character required, but once he called action, Hayworth displayed a smoldering sexuality

---

32 Coincidentally, in 1931 Barthelmess had starred in *The Last Flight*, the film version of John Monk Saunders's stage play *Nikki* (1931). Quite likely the use of the name "Cary Lockwood" by Barthelmess in the Warner Bros. movie was one of the reasons why Paramount nixed Archie Leach's suggestion of the name for himself.

33 Hayworth had briefly been considered to play the part of Julia in *Holiday* (1938), but it was decided that she was still too inexperienced an actress to hold her own in scenes with Grant, let alone Hepburn.

on camera that was exactly what Hawks was looking for in Judy. She got the part.

The cast was fleshed out with such learned character actors as Thomas Mitchell, Sig Rumann and Noah Beery, Jr. (who, although only 25 years of age at the time, was already a nearly two-decade long movie veteran in Hollywood.) Filming began on December 19, 1938 and was set to conclude by mid-February . . . although no one who knew how Howard Hawks worked could have possibly believed he would stay on that timetable. Not surprisingly, he didn't, instead running 31 days over schedule.

As the film opens, Bonnie Lee disembarks from a cargo ship in the (fictional) South American port of Barranca, on her way to Panama, where she hopes to find work as an entertainer. There she meets two pilots for a small local airline that primarily flies cargo and mail on a dangerous route over the Andes Mountains. Discovering they are fellow Americans she invites them for a drink, and soon enough meets Geoff Carter, who runs the air service for Dutchy, the kindly owner of the local watering hole, who also owns the ramshackle airline.

Since her ship won't be departing until 4:00 the following morning, Bonnie agrees to have dinner with one of the flyers, Joe, as soon as he gets back from a mail run. But a sudden fog rolls in as he's returning; he hits a tree as he tries to land and cracks up his plane and is killed. Bonnie, who witnesses the crash, is horrified, and then shocked that Joe's fellow pilots act as if nothing has happened, even going so far as to say they don't know anyone named Joe.

In the cantina Bonnie is distraught as everyone drinks and laughs. When the steak that Joe had earlier ordered to be waiting for him when he arrived is brought to the table, Geoff starts to eat it. Bonnie angrily slaps him and stalks off, and Geoff follows to explain the facts of life in his corner of the world, namely that Joe is dead, and no amount of weeping and moaning will ever bring him back. In the meantime, the pilots must keep doing their jobs. Unspoken but clear is the fact that every pilot knows that odds are, sooner or later they'll be killed as well.

As Bonnie gets to know Geoff better, she recognizes that his fatalism stems in part from having his heart broken. "Well," she says, "someone must have given you an awful beating once." He opens up about a woman he loved, but she left him, because she couldn't take the uncertainty of knowing if each flight would be his last. An obvious attraction sparks between Geoff and Bonnie, and he suggests she comes over to his place to 'look at pictures', but when she agrees, he catches himself and suggests she go to her ship instead and then sail away from Barranca forever.

Instead, Bonnie lets the ship sail without her, and she stays in Barranca . . . much to Geoff's annoyance, and he makes it clear he never asked her to stay. A new pilot arrives, Bat MacPherson, but when the other pilots learn that he bailed on his mechanic . . . who just happened to have been the brother of Kid Dabb, one of their own pilots . . . Bat is shunned by them. Complicating things further for Geoff is that Bat's young wife, Judy, is his former lover, whom he still carries a torch for. The sexual tension between them is palpable.

Bad weather threatens a vital flight, which must be completed for the airline to get an all-important contract that will save it from failure. Given the danger involved, Geoff won't assign any other pilot to make the run, he'll do it himself, with Kid as his co-pilot. Bonnie, who is now in love with Geoff, refuses to let him go, and inadvertently shoots him in the shoulder. With his wound, he's unable to fly, and Bat takes the flight instead.

The plane is struck by a flock of condors in the fog, destroying two of the plane's three engines, with one of the condors crashing through the windshield, striking Kid and breaking his neck. As Bat struggles to get the plane back to the field, Kid urges him to save himself and bail out, but MacPherson refuses. He manages to crash land the plane on the runway, and as Kid lays dying, he tells the others how Bat refused to abandon him. MacPherson is now accepted by the other pilots as one of their own.

As the weather clears, Geoff (his gunshot wound now bandaged) prepares to make the delivery and win the contract. Bonnie informs him she won't be there when he gets back . . . that since he never asked her to stay, she's leaving. "I'm hard to get, Geoff," she tells him. "All you have to do is ask me." But he still can't bring himself to say the words. Instead, he suggests they let a coin toss decide . .

. heads she stays. The coin comes up heads, but she won't abide by it, insisting she must hear the words to know that he truly means it. He hands her the coin as a souvenir, says goodbye and leaves for his plane. She finally looks at the coin and realizes it's a trick double-headed quarter that had been Kid's. She rushes outside to see Geoff taking off on his dangerous flight, but she knows at last that he wants her, and she'll be there when he returns.

For moviegoers who had only truly begun paying close attention to Grant since the success of *Topper* (1937), *Only Angels Have Wings* was unlike anything else they had seen from him. His Geoff Carter was a hard and damaged man, with nary a trace of the light-heartedness of Jerry Wariner and Johnny Case. There are a few brief moments of semi-humor, such as when Grant gets to nod toward his beloved music hall during a cantina sing-a-long, or the running gag of his always asking for a match. There's also a passing glimpse of the Hawksian overlapping dialogue, as Geoff goes over the details of an air route with Bat while simultaneously a local doctor exuberantly quotes Shakespeare (in Spanish). Otherwise, the film is played as straight drama (with more than a few dollops of melodrama, to be sure).

Additionally, for all her vexations with the role, Jean Arthur is surprisingly successful as Bonnie Lee, much of the time. Although with her fresh-scrubbed pertness and neatly pressed clothes, she comes off more as if she's working in Earl Carroll's Vanities on Broadway, rather than being a down on her luck second-string performer struggling to find work in South American backwater towns[34].

As he had with *Bringing Up Baby* (1938), Hawks made up much of the time lost to going over schedule by editing the film as it was being shot (which was a prime reason why he opted to shoot it sequentially). Therefore, he had a finished print ready for Columbia's bi-coastal premieres of the film less than two weeks after the last retake was done. It debuted in Los Angeles at the Pantages on May 10th, and the next day in New York at Radio City Music Hall and was met with praise by critics on both sides of the coun-

---

34 One can only wistfully wonder what Barbara Stanwyck or Joan Blondell might have done with the part.

try. Even Nugent of *The Times* applauded it. For several reviewers, Grant's performance was the first time that he wasn't simply a *personality*, but rather had displayed genuine ability as a serious actor. The film did excellent business across the country and was one of Columbia's biggest hits of the year.

The studio's advertising made much of this being the first time that Cary Grant and Jean Arthur had co-starred together, and played up the film's "breathless romance," rather than its tense drama. Even the film poster showed a smiling Grant and Arthur cuddling side by side. But probably Columbia's most unusual marketing tactic was to assemble Grant, Arthur, Barthelmess, Mitchell and Hayworth to recreate their roles in a radio adaptation on the *Lux Radio Theatre* a mere two weeks after the film opened. Generally, the studios didn't allow adaptations until long after ... in some cases a year or more ... a film had finished its theatrical run, so as to not compete with the movie and impact its box office. But Columbia gambled that in this instance, hearing an abridged version on the air would help boost ticket sales, and they were right.

Coming in on the wake of *Gunga Din*'s spectacular success, *Only Angels Have Wings* helped solidify Grant's hard-earned stardom, and left the public anxious to see what he would do next.

⁂

Oh, by the way, will you marry me?: *In Name Only*

Given the tremendous success of *Gunga Din*, it would have seemed the obvious thing for RKO to put Grant in another adventure film where he would essentially be playing Archie Cutter again. Instead, they initially opted for a comedy, *Bachelor Mother* (1939), co-starring Ginger Rogers. But for unclear reasons, Grant was soon replaced by David Niven.

Then, perhaps to make up for the fact that he hadn't been able to do *Love Affair* (1939), the studio instead gave him another romantic melodrama, *In Name Only* (1939).

His co-star would be Carole Lombard, a fellow former Paramount contractee (she and Grant had co-starred in *The Eagle and the Hawk* in 1933) who, like Grant, had gone freelance, and was now the highest paid actress in Hollywood, earning $150,000 per film. She could not have failed to notice that the plot of the movie bore more than a passing resemblance to her own real-life situation with Clark Gable, who desperately wanted to end his loveless marriage with Ria Langham and wed Lombard, but his wife refused to allow him a divorce. In fact, that's probably the very reason she accepted the role[35].

After *Only Angels Have Wings*, Grant was eager to do another dark drama, and RKO promised him that *In Name Only* would be just that. But when he finally received the script by Richard Sherman (based on the 1934 novel *Memory of Love* by Bessie Breuer, a property RKO had earlier bought as a possible vehicle for Katharine Hepburn), he was disappointed to discover it was little more than the typically sudsy soap opera, albeit written with more intelligence and sensitivity than most others. Such 'women's pictures' were a staple of Hollywood fare, and they were by their nature showcases for actresses, with the male leads rarely having the opportunity to shine. In this film, the emotional weight of the story would be carried largely by Lombard, as well as by Kay Francis, playing the spiteful wife, which meant that the attention of the viewers would remain riveted on them. And while it would be impossible to ever ignore Cary Grant on the screen, he realized from the start this would not be his picture.

He certainly made the most of what he was given, and it was easy for filmgoers to understand just why Lombard's character falls so deeply in love with him. In later years, some observers would dismiss certain performances by Grant by saying, "He's just playing Cary Grant," which is to say he didn't do much deep acting so much as just rely on his unique charm and impeccable timing to carry off his role. In *In Name Only*, it could perhaps be said he was "just playing Cary Grant."

The film opens with Julie Eden fishing in a pond, when a stranger riding on horseback, Alec Walker, approaches. After some sarcastically flirtatious banter, they share the sandwiches which Julie has

---

35 Shortly before *In Name Only* began shooting, Gable finally obtained his divorce, and immediately afterward married Lombard.

brought, and he promises to bring the lunch tomorrow (in Hollywood parlance, this is known as a 'meet cute').

Alec and Julie then begin to meet every day, and mutual affection grows between them. She is a widowed commercial artist raising a five-year-old daughter and renting a small home on the estate owned by the Walker family. She knows he's a Walker himself, but what he doesn't reveal is that he's married.

His marriage to Maida has proven to be a loveless one, as she's only interested in his wealth and the social position being Mrs. Alec Walker provides her. As Alec finds himself falling in love with Julie, he decides at last to divorce his wife. However, Maida coldly refuses to allow him his freedom, and she is so craftily cunning, she has little trouble convincing his parents that Julie is a gold-digging homewrecker who has set out to ruin Alec and Maida's happy marriage. Of course, Maida presents herself to others as thoroughly loving and virtuous.

Finally realizing that so long as Maida won't release him, she and Alec can have no future together, and Julie breaks off their relationship. On Christmas Eve, tormented at having seemingly lost Julie and true happiness forever, Alec gets drunk and passes out in front of an open window, and over the course of the cold winter night contracts pneumonia. As he hovers on the brink of life and death, Julie comes to his bedside, and the doctor tells her that his only hope is that he has something to live for, so that he has the willpower to fight against his illness. Julie then lies to Alec, telling him that Maida will give him a divorce so that they can be together at last.

Now Maida arrives and Julie confronts her. The wife freely admits she doesn't love Alec, only his money, and that she has been gleefully deceiving everyone. But what Maida doesn't know is that Alec's mother and father have made a timely arrival, and they have overheard her confession. Her duplicity revealed, Maida's hold on Alec is broken, and the film ends on an auteur's visual note: defeated, Maida stands in silence as Julie rejoins Alec in his hospital room, closing the door on her and all her cruel machinations in a symbolic scene of love triumphant.

This tidy happy ending was a last-minute alteration to the script. Originally, instead of contracting pneumonia, Julie and Alec learn that she is pregnant with his child. But he also learns that he is dying of an unspecified disease and has only six more months to live. Rather than subject Julie to the heartbreak of caring for him until his death, he breaks things off with her and sends her away, and thus the story ends as pure tragedy. However, the Motion Picture Production Code, known more familiarly as the Hays Office, strongly objected to this scenario, as having Julie be pregnant suggests that she and Alec had slept together, and pre-marital sex was forbidden by the Code.

Indeed, the sanctity of marriage itself was inviolable under the Code, but the film cannily evades that edict by taking advantage of another rule, that evil must not be rewarded. Allowing the thoroughly wicked Maida to win and keep her hooks in Alec breaks that pious regulation, so in this very rare instance, the MPPC consented to the divorce.

Grant couldn't possibly have been overly enthusiastic about making this film, not after the creative personal triumphs of the past two years. But whatever his disenchantment, it was undoubtedly mitigated by working alongside such an excellent cast, which included not only Lombard and Francis, but also Charles Coburn, Jonathan Hale, and young Peggy Ann Garner as Julie's daughter, Ellen. He was almost certainly quite happy with the $100,000 salary he was receiving for this production.

John Cromwell was an experienced and nuanced director whose work here helped elevate this film above its mawkish melodrama, and drew a fine performance in particular from Lombard. Between his deft work and the star power of the leads, upon its release in August, *In Name Only* was a strong box office success, eventually earning nearly $1,500,000 against a $700,000 budget. After the financial disappointments of 1938, it would appear that by 1939, the name of Cary Grant on the marquee was money in the bank.

Somewhat surprisingly, considering that such 'weepers' were so often dismissed by reviewers, many critics loved this film, with even Nugent at *The New York Times* praising it.

In June, once filming on *In Name Only* wrapped, Grant and a now fully recovered Brooks set sail for England aboard the S.S. Normandie. He was returning not only to again visit with his mother, but also to accompany Phyllis as she traveled to the U.K. in order to make a film, *Lucky to Me* (1939). Her Hollywood career was faltering after a few hopeful flickers, and Twentieth Century-Fox had recently released her from her contract. She honestly wasn't that upset over it, as her acting was more of a lark than a lifetime career choice. Truth be told, she'd much rather be Mrs. Cary Grant than a film starlet[36].

That however was seeming less and less likely. Although Grant would still speak of marriage, he continued to refuse to commit. Brooks was growing weary of this game of cat and mouse. And her mother was still advocating hard for Phyllis to be done with him and find someone who would marry her. Inevitably, their relationship began to fray.

They arrived in an England that was girding itself for war. Londoners were digging trench shelters in Hampstead Heath in anticipation of German bombs falling on them, and the government was distributing gas masks to the populace as fast as they could be produced in preparation for the expected poison gas attacks. Hitler had by this time completely discarded the Munich Agreement and gobbled up the entirety of Czechoslovakia, and it didn't take a clairvoyant to predict that the next target of the Nazis would be Poland. Abandoning at last the futile policy of appeasement, the governments in London and Paris announced that they would aid Poland should it come under attack, thus setting the stage for another battlefield conflagration with Germany barely twenty years after the conclusion of the supposed "War to End all Wars."

As Brooksie reported to Elstree Studios to shoot her film, Grant went to Bristol. The time he spent with Elsie was much less strained on this visit than in the past, although it was not without

---

36 Brooks would continue to appear in films, mostly 'B' movies, until 1945, when she retired from acting to marry Torbert Macdonald, who later served for twenty years in the U.S. House of Representatives. John F. Kennedy, a longtime friend of Torbert, was the godfather of one of their four children.

its difficulties. She still refused to move to California to be near him, but Grant was adamant that his mother should get away from Bristol...with its docks and factories, it was a prime target for Hitler's bombers ... and he toured the countryside with her searching for a house she might like. But although she enjoyed their jaunts, as the Southwest summertime landscape was awash with rolling green hills and the colorful vibrancy of Maltese-crosses, foxgloves and red campions, she was nonetheless unmovable in her declaration that she would not leave Bristol. Finally, a compromise was reached between them: Grant would secure Elsie a new home in Bristol, but far enough away from the likely military targets that she (and he) shouldn't have to worry about a German bomb falling through her roof.

※

The likelihood of war weighed heavy on Grant's mind. First and foremost had to be the question: *What would he do if England went to war?* Still vivid in his mind were the images of wounded British Tommies on the Bristol docks in the last war, awful memories that he could never shake. That alone had a powerful pull for staying in America and staying out of the fighting. Yet while Cary Grant was a celebrated citizen of Hollywood, Archie Leach was still a subject of the British Crown, and there would likely be a widespread public sentiment in Britain that every able-bodied Englishman should fight for king and country. At 35 years of age, Grant was still young enough ... and given his exercise regimen, certainly more than fit enough ... to put on a uniform and pick up a rifle.

There was no easy answer for him. He could only hope that the diplomats and politicians managed to find a peaceful solution before Europe, and perhaps the entire world, was plunged into bloodshed again.

On the first of September, the diplomats and politicians no longer had a say in the matter, as Hitler's forces swarmed across the Polish border and rolled incessantly Eastward. Germany had shocked its enemies by securing a non-aggression pact with the Soviet Union, thus shattering the hopes of Britain and France that Russia would join them in an alliance against the Germans, and between them Adolph Hitler and Josef Stalin carved up Poland.

War was declared, armies were mobilized and then . . . nothing. The French sat behind their defensive Maginot Line, the British sent 150,000 troops to join them, but the German Wehrmacht made no direct moves against the Allies. Other than a few indeterminate land skirmishes and some scuffles at sea between the Royal Navy and the Kriegsmarine, a months-long period of non-hostilities, dubbed the "Phony War", characterized the (non-)conflict. Hopes that peace could still be salvaged rose.

Now back in California, Grant took a wait-and-see position for the moment. Others however weren't being quite so passive. David Niven, prior to coming to America and getting into the movies, had served in the British Army, and a few weeks after the war began, he returned home and rejoined the service, later calling this act, "the only unselfish thing I have ever done for humanity." And he wasn't the only one of Grant's friends to don khaki, as Robert Coote enlisted in the Royal Canadian Air Force. Basil Rathbone attempted to join the army, but at 47 was rejected for being too old. In a fit of patriotic zeal, Charles Boyer rushed to Paris and enlisted in the French Army, serving for three months before the Daladier government realized who he actually was, mustered him out, and told him to go back to Hollywood and make movies that convinced Americans to join the fight.

Grant joined a small contingent of British expatriates . . . Sir Cedric Hardwicke, Laurence Olivier, producer Herbert Wilcox and himself . . . on a trip to Washington, D.C. for a private meeting with Lord Lothian, the British Ambassador to the United States. Their flight hit a thunderstorm that tossed the craft violently through the air, and Grant tried to calm Wilcox's frazzled nerves by singing his beloved English music hall songs. At the embassy, Lothian had a message for them to take back to the British film colony in Hollywood: stay where you are and make movies that promote the valor of England. He said that the English actors, directors and screenwriters were in an invaluable location to disseminate pro-British propaganda to the American people, not to mention morale-boosting motion pictures for the citizens of the Allied nations. They were far more valuable to the crown in Hollywood than they could ever be in uniform.

For Grant, that largely settled the issue. He stayed in Hollywood making films (and indeed in 1942 became a U.S. citizen, also taking that opportunity to legally change his name to Cary Grant at last)[37]. He would donate his full salary from a couple of his pictures to the war effort, entertain wounded troops in military hospitals, and tour the United States raising millions of dollars by promoting the sale of war bonds. The closest he would ever get to fighting the Axis powers was in war films such as *Once Upon a Honeymoon* (1942), *Destination Tokyo* (1943) and *Father Goose* (1964).

Throughout the war, the German Luftwaffe dropped some 919 tons of bombs on Bristol, killing 1299 Bristolians . . . including several members of Grant's extended family, as well as friends he had grown up with. During the Blitz Elsie Leach, still stubbornly staying in Bristol and maintaining the quintessential British stiff upper lip, sent her son a telegram: DON'T WORRY ABOUT MOTHER PULLED THROUGH LAST WAR.

---

37 There have long been rumors that Grant did secret espionage work for the British government in Hollywood, reporting on actors and others in the industry who had pro-Nazi, or at least anti-British, sympathies. This was quite possibly true. It's known that a number of Brits in the U.S. were asked to undertake such surveillance by their government. Film producer Alexander Korda, dispatched from London to Hollywood by Winston Churchill himself to make pro-English films with the American studios, was also closely tied in with the British intelligence service, and may well have been Grant's espionage overseer. Korda was knighted by King George VI in 1942 for unspecified contributions to the war effort. In 1947, the King awarded Grant himself the King's Medal for Service in the Cause of Freedom.

1940

The last man who said that to me was Archie Leach: *His Girl Friday*

"The finest modern dialogue that had been written," is how Howard Hawks described *The Front Page* (1931). His appreciation of Ben Hecht and Charles MacArthur's influential stage play extended beyond mere esteem to outright theft of the basic story for *Gunga Din* (aided and abetted by Hecht and MacArthur themselves, of course). As far as Hawks was concerned, the play's crackling quick-fire language was so impeccable, it was virtually bulletproof no matter who was speaking it.

To prove it, one night in 1938 he and his girlfriend, Nancy "Slim" Keith, were hosting a small dinner party, and for entertainment after the meal, Howard and Slim read scenes from the play for their guests, with Hawks as editor Walter Burns, and Slim as reporter Hildy Johnson[38]. Either that night or shortly thereafter, it dawned on Hawks that a new motion picture version of the play (it had been filmed once before in 1931 by director Lewis Milestone for producer Howard Hughes, starring Adolph Menjou as Burns and Pat O'Brian as Johnson. The movie was a box office hit and is credited by many film historians as a pioneer entry in the screwball comedy genre) could succeed if the part of Hildy was changed from a man to a woman. Hawks phoned his friend Hecht and asked him if he minded the gender switch, and Hecht gave his blessing. "I think it's a great idea," the playwright told him.

During the shooting of *Only Angels Have Wings* (1939*)*, Hawks went to Columbia's Harry Cohn and told him he had an idea for Cary Grant's next film, a new version of *The Front Page*. Cohn

---
[38] Or so the legend goes. In some versions, it's a woman other than Slim Keith. In others, there never was a reading at a dinner party or anywhere else.

immediately liked it, and said that Grant would make a great Hildy Johnson, and then suggested newspaper columnist Walter Winchell as Burns. Hawks immediately doused the mogul's enthusiasm by informing him that no, Grant would play Burns, and a woman would be Johnson; he may have mentioned Ginger Rogers as a good choice for the part, but Cohn wasn't hearing him any longer. He thought the director was either out of his tree, or else was pulling his leg, and either way he didn't have time to waste on such nonsense.

Hawks, in his calm and quiet manner, talked Cohn down from his angry peak and, laying out his vision of the story, was able to bring the studio head around again to liking the idea. Columbia bought the film rights and announced it as their next project with Cary Grant.

The obvious choices to write the screenplay were Hecht and MacArthur, but they were otherwise occupied at the time; Hecht was officially scripting *Wuthering Heights* (1939), *It's a Wonderful World* (1939) and *Lady of the Tropics* (1939), and unofficially co-writing *Gone with the Wind* (1939), and MacArthur was directing one of his and Hecht's plays, *Ladies and Gentlemen* (1939), on Broadway.

So, Hawks turned to Gene Fowler, who had been a friend of and fellow reporter with Hecht and MacArthur in both Chicago and New York, and likewise had come to Hollywood to write for films. He had worked uncredited on Hawks' *Twentieth Century* (1934) and had also made uncredited contributions to *The Front Page*. However, Fowler considered the original script to be sacrosanct, taking offense at the very notion of making Hildy Johnson a woman, and declined the invitation to work on this version.

The 1931 film script bore differences from the play, primarily to structure the story better for a motion picture. Those alterations were the work of screenwriter Charles Lederer, himself a former journalist. Hawks now reached out to him, and Lederer was interested in the opportunity to return to the story and intrigued by the director's plans for Hildy. Lederer signed on.

Lederer and Hawks began working on the script . . . and found themselves joined for a time by Hecht, who despite his scripting workload on other films, could not resist the chance to play around with these characters once again, although his contribution would remain uncredited. Hawks' concept of the script would be that it should take *The Front Page*'s fast-paced dialogue and make it even more rapid-fire, so much so that characters would actually talk over one another. This blatantly violated an unwritten rule of filmmaking, that dialogue should be enunciated so that the audience should have no difficulty hearing it clearly, and conversational lines should be spoken with enough separation between them that the viewers can cognitively grasp what they are hearing — but for this film, Hawks cared for none of that.

It was Lederer who devised the new dynamic between Burns and Hildy that drives their conflict. It had been said by reviewers in the past that the relationship between the editor and reporter in the original play was more a platonic love affair than that of boss/employee. The screenwriter took that to the next level by having Burns and Hildy (the full name changed from the masculine Hildebrand to the feminine Hildegard) be a recently divorced husband and wife.

While Hawks may have proclaimed that Hecht and MacArthur's original dialogue was superior to any other, that didn't stop him and Lederer, once they really got rolling on the script, to throw out old lines and concoct new ones. Hawks reasoned that he wasn't doing a straight remake of the 1931 film, but rather adapting it for what was in many ways an entirely different film. The script would be tweaked continuously throughout the shoot, and of course the director encouraged his main actors to improvise as they wished.

While Grant was set right from the start, and other actors ... Ralph Bellamy, Gene Lockhart, Roscoe Karns ... were quickly added, the key role of Hildy Johnson herself proved much more difficult to cast. Harry Cohn had again wanted Jean Arthur, but she had no interest in ever working with Hawks again. Ginger Rogers ... Carole Lombard ... Claudette Colbert ... Irene Dunne ... Joan Crawford ... each of them declined the role. Presumably they were intimidated by the busy and demanding script, and not reluctant to work with either Grant or Hawks.

Just days before filming was set to commence, Cohn took executive action. He had recently seen *The Women* (1939) and was impressed by one of the actresses, Rosalind Russell. He called MGM and arranged for her to be loaned to Columbia. Russell was vacationing on the East Coast and hurried back to Hollywood by train. Just before she departed for California, *The New York Times* ran an item that listed all the actresses who had already refused the part, and added that Columbia had to settle for Russell, who they hadn't really wanted. She'd already heard industry chatter about how many others had turned down this role, so she was under no illusions that she was Howard Hawks' first choice. In fact, she later liked to say she was lucky to have been his fifteenth choice, but the insinuation by *The Times* (she presumed the gossip was leaked by someone at Columbia, or perhaps Hawks himself) that she was being forced on Hawks infuriated her. In point of fact, Hawks wasn't enthusiastic at all about having Russell imposed on him (he hadn't yet seen *The Women*, so he wasn't very familiar with her work), and his reluctance seemed justified when she came to the studio to meet with him for the first time, looking very unglamorous in an old dress, her hair still damp from the morning swim she had taken; no one would mistake her at first glance for a Hollywood star, he must have thought.

Despite her privileged upbringing, Russell prided herself in being what the vernacular of the day would call a 'brassy broad', and she was unafraid of confrontation. Her first words to Hawks were, "You didn't want me for this, did you?" The director's reply, perhaps more to reassure himself than her, was, "It'll be all right, you'll be fine."

Once shooting began, she didn't feel fine. Hawks' unwillingness to give detailed directions or feedback confounded her. She took Grant aside and asked, "What is it with this guy?" Grant assured her she was doing just fine, and that if Hawks didn't like her performance, he would tell her, but that still didn't satisfy her, so she went to Hawks himself in exasperation and asked him to please tell her what she should do. He just looked at her with his dark eyes, and in his quiet voice said, "You just keep pushin' him around the way you're doin'."

With that, Russell came to understand Hawks and his style, and furthermore better grasped the character of Hildy Johnson. She wasn't just supposed to be a sassy gal…she was feminine yes, but also tough, smart, and unafraid to stand her ground. She was one of the boys, and fiercer than most of them.

The film opens with Hildy returning to *The Morning Post* from the extended vacation she had taken following her divorce from Walter Burns, the paper's cynical editor. Burns is happy to have his best reporter back, but she tells him she's quitting, and what's more she's getting married again, to a man she met on vacation. Burns is taken aback for a moment, but quickly schemes a situation where Hildy can cover a story one last time. She's reluctant but her fiancé, Bruce Baldwin (Ralph Bellamy, once again playing the hapless other man to Cary Grant), urges her to do it after Burns agrees to take out a $100,000 life insurance policy from insurance agent Bruce in exchange.

Hildy heads down to the county jail, where a milquetoast bookkeeper named Earl Williams is about to be executed for having shot and killed an African-American police officer. The mayor is pushing hard for the hanging to happen quickly because he's in a tight re-election race, and he hopes to draw enough votes from the black wards as a result of the execution to retain his office. As events unfold, the incompetent sheriff inadvertently helps Williams escape, and while all the other reporters rush out of the press room to cover the story (following an amusing bit where each reporter calls their paper and successively top one another with exaggerated "facts" of the escape), Hildy remains behind…and is taken hostage by the armed Williams when he enters the room to hide. Hildy's reporter instincts kick in and she completely forgets about Bruce (who now realizes she can never give up being a reporter, not even for him, and he gloomily heads for home in Albany, New York along with his mother) as she calms down Williams and convinces him she won't turn him in, then calls Burns and tells him get down to the jail immediately. She hides Williams in a roll top desk and later they try to smuggle him out of the jail, but he's discovered, and the mayor orders the sheriff to arrest Burns and Hildy. Just then it's revealed that the Governor had earlier signed a reprieve for Williams on psychiatric grounds, and that the mayor had hidden that fact for his own political purposes.

Shortly before filming began, Hawks took Lederer's script and gave it to another screenwriter, Morrie Ryskind, and asked him to make suggestions. Ryskind concocted a new ending which saw Hildy and Burns getting remarried in the newsroom, only to immediately erupt into a rowdy verbal argument, while one of the other characters benignly smiles and says, "I think it's gonna turn out alright this time." Pleased with himself, Ryskind went to lunch in the Columbia commissary and enthusiastically shared his ending with the other writers at the table. A week or so later he was shocked to discover that one of those writers appropriated the entire ending and incorporated it into the script *he* was writing, and that the filched scene had just been shot for that film. Now forced to come up with a new ending, Ryskind had Burns propose to Hildy and promise to take her on the honeymoon to Niagara Falls that they never got around to the first time they were wed. As a happy bonus, there's a labor strike in Albany they can stop off at to cover, and Burns mordantly asks, "I wonder if Bruce can put us up?"

Having learned his lesson about the cutthroat nature of Hollywood screenwriting, Ryskind did not share this scene with any of the other writers in the commissary.

Throughout the story, Walter Burns is repeatedly contriving schemes to derail Bruce Baldwin, including setting him up for arrest several times on charges ranging from theft (repurposing a stolen watch bit from the original play), to "mashing," to carrying counterfeit money. His henchman in this is Diamond Louie, a hoodlum who Burns keeps in his employ for just such jobs. Louie is played to strong comedic effect by Abner Biberman, who had previously played the murderously menacing Chota in *Gunga Din*. On the mashing charge, Louie uses his saucy peroxide blonde moll to set up Bruce, and when Hildy angrily derides her as an "albino," Louie takes umbrage at this, insisting, "She ain't no albino, she was born right here in this country."

Bellamy enjoyed working on the film, in particular reteaming with Grant. However, he feared that after so many roles such as this, he was in danger of being typecast. Those fears were made more real not terribly long after making *His Girl Friday* (1940), when he was visiting with producer Mark Hellinger at his Warner Brothers office. When Hellinger took a call, Bellamy happened to glance at a paper on the desk and spotted his own name written on it. Reading it more closely he discovered it was a character list for a film synopsis, and he was mentioned not as a potential actor for the film, but rather as a specific type of character himself: "A charming but naïve fellow…a typical Ralph Bellamy part." Mortified to learn he had become a cliché for a sap within the movie industry, Bellamy pulled up stakes from Hollywood and headed for New York, where he launched a long and terrifically successful career on the Broadway stage, returning afterward to films only when it suited him, and the role was not a "Ralph Bellamy part."

Russell learned quickly that Hawks encouraged improvisation, and with Cary Grant, she was working with a master at the quippy ad-lib. While filming their first scene together, which not surprisingly for this film featured an argument between Hildy and Burns, Russell decided on the spur of the moment to angrily throw her purse at Grant. He managed to duck under it and verbally shot back with, "You used to be better than that." Hawks loved it and it stayed in the picture.

In another instance, Grant was caught by surprise by one of Russell's extemporaneous moments, and he looked off-camera to the director and asked, "Is she going to do that?" Hawks left all of that in the film as well.

The most famous moments of improvisation in the film resulted from a pair of in-jokes. In one scene, while on the telephone describing how Bruce Baldwin looks, Burns says, "He looks like that fellow in the movies…Ralph Bellamy." Harry Cohn hated that when he saw the rushes, but Bellamy himself told him he thought it was hilarious, and he asked that it be left in the movie. Most memorable of all, later in the film Burns says, "Listen, the last man who said that to me was Archie Leach just a week before he cut his throat."[39]

---

39 It wouldn't be the last time it made its way into a Cary Grant film. In *Arsenic and Old Lace* (1944), a gravestone in a cemetery scene bears the name 'Archie Leach'.

Roz Russell was proving that she could more than hold her own with Grant in terms of improvisations . . . but Grant was starting to grow suspicious that her witticisms weren't quite as spontaneous as they seemed. Finally, he took her aside and asked how she was always so ready with a perfect wisecrack, and Russell confessed that she had hired a writer to work with her and punch up her lines with more comedy. Grant thought that was marvelous and kept her secret.

Grant and Russell were both concerned that all the overlapping dialogue would make it too difficult for the audience to follow what was being said, but Hawks instead encouraged them to really pile it on. He let them in on his strategy: he was building a specific mood with the rat-a-tat conversations, but then when the scene between Hildy and Earl Johnson came, she would play that so slowly and quietly, the mood would dramatically shift, and the silence would bowl the audience over. Then they'd jump right back into the dialogue roller coaster all the way to the final scene.

Hawks also encouraged Grant to really get forceful in a scene where Burns pushes Hildy down onto a couch. Grant was reluctant, concerned he might injure Russell. "Well, I don't want to kill the woman," he said. Hawks quietly mulled it over for a few moments, and then replied, "Try killing her."

Perhaps it was the rapid pace of the dialogue, but filming moved along briskly, and when the final scene was shot on November 21st the film was a mere seven days over schedule (something of a minor miracle for a Hawks production). Columbia ran a few sneak previews in December to audience acclaim, and *His Girl Friday* formally premiered at Radio City in New York on January 11th of 1940, and one week later went into nationwide release. It was an immediate hit and was held over for the all-important second week at Radio City.

The success of *His Girl Friday* solidified Rosalind Russell's new status as a major star, and for the next twenty years she continued to headline in motion pictures, picking up no fewer than four Academy Award nominations for Best Actress along the way. It was her participation in the film that led to an even more momentous change in her life.

Frederick Brisson had been born in Denmark, the son of Carl Brisson, a musical comedy star in Britain and throughout Europe as well. After being educated in England Freddie opted to follow his father into show business, but not as a performer. He worked booking acts for the stage, got into theatrical and film promotion, and even dabbled in producing movies. By the late 1930s he was well established as a talent agent and had built important ties with Hollywood that allowed him to import a number of American stars across the Atlantic to appear in British films. In 1939, Frank W. Vincent invited Brisson to move to Los Angeles and be a partner in his agency.

Freddie and Cary Grant had met several years earlier during one of Grant's visits back to the U.K. and had hit it off (it certainly helped that Grant was such a fan of Freddie's father, Carl), and as Brisson would now be working with his own manager, Grant invited him to come stay at the actor's own home until he could get settled in Hollywood.

As he sailed across the ocean, Brisson discovered that apparently the ship had only one movie to show, and it ran very nearly continuously around the clock. For the first few days of the voyage, as he settled into a preferred spot on the deck to relax and read, he could hear the sound from the film playing from the nearby theater. After repeated listens, he had come to particularly hate the very sound of one specific actress's voice, and finally he decided he may as well go in and watch the film, since he was already so familiar with its dialogue. Besides, he was curious who the actress whose voice annoyed him was.

The film was *The Women* (1939), and the actress was Rosalind Russell. And watching the film, Brisson was astonished to soon discover that rather than hating her, he was becoming fascinated by the American actress. By the time the ship docked, and he had taken a cross-country train trip to California, he was determined to meet her. He was surprised and delighted when he shared this information with his host and was told that Grant was in fact just starting a film with Russell. Brisson implored Grant to make an introduction for him, and the actor said he would see what he could do.

However, his way of doing something was rather roundabout. Each day on the set, Grant would ask Russell, "Do you know Freddie Brisson?" and each day Russell would tell him she did not, but he would never go on to explain just who Freddie Brisson was. She quickly began to suspect this was some unfathomable gag that Grant was playing on her. Then one evening Grant and Russell had made plans to go dancing together. When he arrived at her house to pick her up, he wasn't alone. He gestured to the man standing next to him and said, "This is Freddie Brisson."

Russell and Grant had a great time that night at Ciro's, dancing and telling funny stories amid gales of laughter. It was genuinely the start of a lifelong friendship between the two. Brisson said very little during the evening, and Russell came away singularly unimpressed with him. When Brisson phoned her a few days later to ask for a date, she made up an excuse to beg off. He kept calling every few days, and Russell kept making excuses, until finally after nine months of this, she gave in and agreed to allow him to accompany her to the thoroughbred races. Shortly thereafter she was invited on a sailing excursion to Catalina Island, but none of her friends were available to join her. It was at that moment that Brisson again called, and Russell surprised even herself by asking if he'd like to come along. He did, and they wound up having a wonderful time together.

On October 25th of 1941 Roz Russell married Freddie Brisson, with Cary Grant as their best man.

●●●

While Grant was helping love blossom between Rosalind and Freddie, he was watching it wither on his own vine. His relationship with Phyllis Brooks had grown somewhat strained due to his unwillingness to settle down with her, but they were still committed deeply to one another throughout 1939. In fact, she had finally gotten him to finally agree to marry her, just as soon as he was done filming *His Girl Friday*. However, she had good reason to expect him to back out yet again, as he had insisted that they not publicly announce their engagement.

When the time to marry finally came, Grant presented Brooks with a prenuptial agreement, which in and of itself was not out of the ordinary among film stars. However, this agreement was not so much about his wealth, as it was about two other provisos he had inserted: the first was that Phyllis would give up her acting career and become a full-time wife. This gave her pause, for although her career wasn't exactly setting Hollywood on fire, she was still working steadily, and the money she earned was supporting her family. It was the second stipulation that was the real bombshell, and that was that Phyllis's mother would be barred from ever setting foot inside the Grant home.

This was too much for Phyllis, and she refused to agree to it. After more than two years together, Brooks and Grant split up once and for all.

By the way, how was my funeral?: *My Favorite Wife*

Even before he had begun shooting *His Girl Friday*, Grant had agreed to his next RKO production. The fact that it didn't yet have a script, and indeed he wasn't even sure what the plot was, gave him no pause. That's because this film would be written and directed by Leo McCarey and would co-star Irene Dunne, reuniting the triumvirate of *The Awful Truth* (1937) at last.

But then disaster struck in November of 1939. McCarey, never the safest of drivers, had been drinking, and was racing down the highway from Lake Arrowhead to Los Angeles far in excess of the speed limit when he smashed up his car, nearly killing himself and his passenger, screenwriter Gene Fowler. Among his many injuries, McCarey had a fractured skull and very nearly severed his right arm. When his friend W.C. Fields later visited the director in the hospital, he said he had heard McCarey had rolled his car over three times, and the comic facetiously asked, "Didn't the first time take?"

Although bedridden, McCarey didn't let his near-fatal accident deter him from making the movie on schedule. He began dictating story ideas and assembled several other writers . . . husband and wife playwrights Samuel and Bella Spewack, as well as Garson Kanin, whom McCarey had designated would be the on-site director, carrying out McCarey's instructions from afar . . . to help him write the script.

His initial inspiration for the film that he was for the moment calling *Woman Overboard* was the 1864 poem *Enoch Arden* by Alfred Lord Tennyson, which tells the tale of a sailor who is lost on a desert island for a decade, only to return home to find his wife remarried, and her new husband raising the sailor's children as his own. As a nod to Tennyson, McCarey gave the two lead characters in his script the surname Arden.

The problem was RKO did not hold the film rights to Tennyson's work. Those in fact were presently owned by Columbia, which was at that very moment adapting the poem (combined with the similarly themed play by W. Somerset Maugham, *Too Many Husbands* {1919}) as the Wesley Ruggles-directed *Too Many Husbands* (1940), starring Jean Arthur, Fred MacMurray, and Melvyn Douglas. And indeed, both Harry Cohn and Maugham were threatening lawsuits if RKO proceeded with their film. But McCarey was undeterred, confident that audiences would find his version the better of the two.

As for the potential suits, McCarey advised RKO to simply claim they were adapting Washington Irving's 1819 short story "Rip Van Winkle", which by that point was in the public domain and available for anyone to use.

Because McCarey would not be present on the set, he knew he could not indulge in the kind of daily rewrites he would do while making *The Awful Truth*. Therefore, he worked on preparing a complete script, and although bits would be added or altered as filming progressed, the screenplay was essentially adhered to from start to finish.

Now retitled *My Favorite Wife* (1940), the story is about a woman, Ellen Arden (Dunne), who disappeared seven years before in a shipwreck, and after her husband Nick (Grant) petitions the court to finally declare her dead, he marries his fiancée, Bianca (Gail Patrick). It is only then that Ellen is rescued and returns home, but instead of having a happy reunion with her husband, she learns he is off on his honeymoon with his second wife.

Ellen follows Nick and Bianca to the lodge where they're staying, where he is shocked to discover that his first wife is still alive. Not at all sure of how to reveal this to Bianca, he says nothing, but with his sudden bizarre behavior (and his unwillingness to consummate their marriage), the new Mrs. Arden is concerned enough about Nick to call in a psychiatrist.

Having learned of Ellen's survival, Nick realizes he still loves her. However the situation becomes more complicated when Nick learns that the man, Stephen Burkett, she was trapped on the island with for all of those years wasn't the timorous older man she was trying to pass off to Nick as being Burkett, but rather a strapping and handsome younger man (played by Randolph Scott in his first film together with Grant since 1932's *Hot Saturday*[40]), who reveals his and Ellen's pet names for one another on the island were Adam and Eve. Nick, not surprisingly, is now consumed by jealousy, and is suspicious of how his wife spent those seven years with Burkett.

Events whirl around the characters until Nick is arrested for bigamy and is hauled before a judge (the selfsame judge who had at the beginning of the film legally declared Ellen dead, and then married Nick and Bianca). The truth now out for all to know, the judge annuls the marriage between Nick and Bianca. However, Ellen is now not certain she wants to reconcile with Nick, and Stephen reveals he is in love with her, and asks her to marry him. In the end, Nick and Ellen reunite in a scene that, by intent, strongly conjures the finale of *The Awful Truth*.

From the very start of filming, Grant had misgivings about the script (which now included contributions from screenwriter John McClain). Not that in his opinion it was bad, nor unfunny, but rather problematic and rather thin. He recalled that the original shooting script of *The Awful Truth* had the same sort of issues, but that McCarey's daily additions and wholesale alterations transformed the entire story for the better. Now of course, McCarey would not be able to make such all-encompassing contributions.

---

40 Unless one also counts *Pirate Party on Catalina Isle* (1935), an MGM short in which Cary and Randolph briefly appear in a non-speaking cameo.

Even when he finally began coming to the set during the last couple of weeks of shooting (against the advice of his doctors, who ordered him to stay in bed and rest), and he started taking a more active role in directing the film, his revisions to the script were far fewer than they had been on the previous movie.

A key problem with the story was that there was no suspense as to which wife Nick would eventually choose. Audiences had no doubt that Ellen would win in the end. As a result of this, while Bianca was never played as callous or hateful (after all if she were, why in the world would Nick have picked her to be the new mother of his two young children?), she was not allowed to gain much sympathy from the audience, even though she is clearly a wronged party in all of this.

Gail Patrick had suggested to McCarey what may seem obvious: that Bianca and Stephen should have gotten together as a couple in the end, leaving the way clear for Nick and Ellen to reunite without recriminations. McCarey, although he was an old hand at weaving sentimentality into his comedy, may have felt this would be just too much of a Hollywood happy ending for everyone. *Enoch Arden*, after all, was a tragedy.

Grant does get to pursue the comic possibilities of his character, largely through double takes and a nice touch of slapstick when his entire body leans to the side as he first spots Ellen just as the door of his elevator is closing.

After a couple of sneak previews in February that did not go as well as hoped... audiences found the last quarter of the film slower and less funny than what had preceded it... McCarey took control of the production and called the actors back to re-shoot some scenes, and he also added more comedic content. Editing the new print together, McCarey was very pleased when preview audiences now raved about it. Although upon its release in May of 1940, while many critics did enjoy it, not many said it was much better than *Too Many Husbands*. And more than a few were disappointed that it wasn't up to the standards set by *The Awful Truth*.

As for Grant, whatever his misgivings were about the script, he made the film for one simple reason: he knew full well that any screwball comedy starring him and Irene Dunne, and with Leo

McCarey's prominent involvement, was going to draw an audience. That meant a bit more to him than usual with this film, because of a new deal he had worked out with RKO. Rather than receive his customary $75,000 he agreed to take only $50,000, but in exchange Grant would receive 2.5% of the profits. As the film earned some $2,000,000 in its first theatrical run in '40, Grant pocketed a cool extra $50,000, and later rereleases (not to mention future sales to television and other mediums) saw Grant continue to earn money from *My Favorite Wife*.

Profit participation was in its way both as rare and radical in Hollywood as was freelancing. It was a trend that most producers would stubbornly resist. Cary Grant was proving to be a vanguard of the future, and by the 1950s, both would be norms within the industry.

❋❋❋

Several months after his break-up with Brooks, Grant began dating Barbara Hutton. Heiress to both the Woolworth five-and-dime store and E.F. Hutton Wall Street brokerage fortunes, Hutton was scathingly dubbed "The Poor Little Rich Girl" by the press for her well-publicized and extravagant lifestyle during the depths of the Great Depression. Hutton and Grant had met aboard the *Normandie* in the summer of 1939, as he sailed home from England. Sharing meals at the captain's table, they had multiple opportunities to converse, and Grant found her not only attractive and charming, but cleverer and more demure than her bad press had led him to expect.

At the time they had begun their relationship, Cary Grant was hardly Barbara Hutton's first brush with Hollywood. She had dated (or at least had trysts) with David Niven, Errol Flynn, Gilbert Roland, Howard Hughes, and even Grant's friend, Frederick Brisson. She'd been married twice, the most recent being to Count Kurt von Haugwitz-Reventlow of Denmark, the father of her young son, Lance.

With their dating now made public, Grant was outraged when the press soon dubbed the duo, "Cash and Cary." The actor bristled at the insinuation that he was only interested in Hutton for her money. In truth, her wealth was very appealing to him, but not because he wanted any of it; it was actually just the opposite. He appreciated the fact that because she had her own fortune, she wasn't interested in claiming any of his (which in any respect was dwarfed by Barbara's estimated worth of $50,000,000). Also pleasing to him was that she wasn't an actress and had no other career that she might insist on maintaining even after marriage.

They swiftly became one of the most famous celebrity couples in America, with their activities shared in gossip columns from coast to coast. Inevitably, some of those columnists soon began to predict that Cary Grant would become Husband No. 3 for Hutton. Many of Grant's friends thought that marriage between the two was highly unlikely. After all, while they greatly enjoyed one another's company for now, they didn't have a great deal in common. Grant was working steadily making movies, which meant he had to be up in the morning before sunrise in order to get to the studio, and frequently didn't return home until 7:00 P.M. or later. That left precious little time to attend cocktail and dinner parties or go dancing...all things which Hutton enjoyed filling her evening hours with. What's more, she preferred to be back in New York City for the fashion season, and summering and sailing on the East Coast. She wasn't terribly interested in the goings on in the movie industry, and he didn't find many of Barbara's interests all that riveting. Matrimony between them would, his friends assured themselves, be a veritable remake of the Randolph Scott-Marion DuPont marriage, and hadn't Grant seen up close just how unfulfilling that union was?

Yet, to the surprise of many, the relationship between Grant and Hutton continued throughout 1940 and beyond[41]...although that

---

41 This brings us to yet another persistent rumor about what Cary Grant may have done for the Allied cause during the war. Supposedly, the Federal Bureau of Investigation secretly asked Grant to surveil Barbara Hutton and her family. This was not so much due to Barbara herself; she was a staunch patriot and donated large sums of money and materials to both the American and British war efforts as well as Charles de Gaulle's Free French forces. However, certain members of her family were known fascist sympathizers, and had allegedly financially supported the pro-Nazi German American Bund before the war, and the FBI was suspicious that at least some of the family's money may have been underwriting Nazi 'fifth column' activities in the U.S.

did not deter him from also quietly spending time with several other ladies, including actresses Carole Landis and Dorothy Lamour.

❂❂❂

Patriots and Tyrants: *The Howards of Virginia*

For years, the consensus in Hollywood was that films set during the American Civil War or the Revolutionary War were sure money-losers, and by and large the studios avoided them. Even the record-shattering success of *Gone with the Wind* failed to spark any sort of a boom for movies about the War Between the States. However, two recent films, *Drums Along the Mohawk* (1939) and *Northwest Passage* (1940), were successful enough to encourage Hollywood to pursue additional productions set in the colonial and Revolutionary periods.

Perhaps surprisingly, Columbia Pictures was among the first to do so. Harry Cohn was never a trendsetting filmmaker, and particularly after *Lost Horizon*, he was loathe to spend huge sums of money adapting sprawling novels to the silver screen. Yet he was also anxious to fully elevate Columbia to a level of prestige comparable to the major studios, and he knew one of the surest ways to do that was to produce expensive epics that won Academy Awards.

Drums Along the Mohawk, *Northwest Passage*, and of course *Gone with the Wind* had all adapted highly successful recent novels of historical fiction, and so Cohn set out looking for a bestselling book of his own to buy. He found it in Elizabeth Page's *The Tree of Liberty*, published in 1939. Expansive is hardly an adequate word to describe it; at 1,000 pages and a half-million words, it tells the story of Matt Howard over the course of some fifty years, from the first stirrings of American independence from the British crown to the end of Thomas Jefferson's tenure as President of the United States. In fact, Jefferson plays an important role throughout the book, as he is the lifelong friend and frequent benefactor of the (fictional) Matt.

There is no evidence yet proving or disproving this theory, as the FBI continues to keep their complete files on both Grant and Hutton during the war years unavailable.

In the story, Matt Howard is an honest, courageous, and hardworking tobacco planter who settles in the frontier of Virginia's Ohio Valley. He is a rugged individualist who adheres to the maxim that the government that governs least, governs best, and is opposed to both taxation and a standing army, and therefore is most unhappy when London imposes both on its colonies. Over the course of the tale, he grows from childhood to adulthood and then into his senior years, courts and marries Jane Peyton, a member of Virginia's planter aristocracy (over the fierce objections of her class-conscious family), fights in the Revolution, sees his new nation born, and his friend Jefferson rise to the highest office in the land.

Overall, there was simply too much story to be fully adapted into a single motion picture, so much of the book's narrative was minimized or jettisoned altogether. As the script by Sidney Buchman (who of course had co-written *Holiday* and done uncredited work on *The Awful Truth*) took shape, it followed the *Gone with the Wind* template by focusing much of its attention on the relationship between Matt and Jane, making the film more romantic drama than historical adventure.

The story, however, remained problematic. At that moment in time, although the U.S. was still officially neutral, a majority of American public sentiment favored Great Britain, so making a movie where the British are the enemy risked alienating many filmgoers, and worse yet, potentially riling up Washington, D.C. as well. Cohn doubtless recalled the story of Robert Goldstein, the movie producer who, in a flush of patriotic pride in 1917, made *The Spirit of '76*, set during the Revolutionary War. But because America was then in the Great War and allied with England, Goldstein's film, which of course by historic necessity had the British as the villains, was seen as pro-German, which had him arrested and imprisoned under the provisions of the wartime Espionage Act.

This resulted in *The Howards of Virginia* (1940) having to tread a very fine line. The ultimate solution was to downplay the idea that it was about Americans fighting for their independence against their British colonial masters, but rather instead focusing on Matt Howard's struggle against the Peytons, who are portrayed as representing everything true Americans ought not to be: haughty, status-obsessed and consumed by their wealth and forever craving more. Naturally, the Peytons are Tories who support the Crown in the War for Independence, while Matt goes off to fight with George Washington's Continental Army.

It proved to be an uncomfortable patchwork of a script, but whatever his concerns about it (and the $1.3 million budget), Cohn had confidence the film could succeed based on three assets it held: it was a popular bestseller with an established audience that presumably would be curious to see the story brought to life on the screen; it was helmed by veteran director Frank Lloyd, who knew his way around a costume drama (as he had proven with *Mutiny on the Bounty* in 1935); and it had Cary Grant.

Grant seemed an unusual choice, not least because of the incongruity of an English actor playing an American colonist who battles the British (and this just months after he had taken his marching orders from Lord Lothian to make pro-British films!) As an actor he didn't feel comfortable doing costume dramas (doubtless a whiff of the failure of *The Toast of New York* {1937} yet lingered in his nostrils). But it still rankled him that he had been denied a chance to be a part of Lloyd's *Mutiny* (1935). And he knew he couldn't keep on making screwball comedies forever...that genre had to fade eventually. Therefore, if he wanted to continue to be a major star, he needed to broaden his acting palate. And so, although he cringed at the very idea of wearing a ponytail wig, he signed on to *The Howards of Virginia*.

He soon wished he hadn't. Even at two hours in length, the film feels bloated and much longer than that. Grant often seems fidgety playing Matt, as if he wants to throw in some pratfalls to break up the monotony. What's more, the romance between Matt and Jane was no Rhett and Scarlett. This was only the second film for Martha Scott, who played Jane, after a successful career on Broadway, and afterward she admitted that she found her performance too "stagey," and not well-suited for the movie. She also confessed that she believed the only reason she got the part was because of her passing resemblance to Barbara Hutton, and Grant had final say over the casting of his leading lady. Some forty years later, running into Scott at an event, Grant apologized to her, blaming himself for the failure of *The Howards of Virginia*, and she found herself having to reassure Cary Grant that he was a good actor, and he hadn't been terrible in the film.

In spite of the challenges in making the film, Scott found the experience of working with Grant to be exhilarating. One of the things that endeared Grant to so many of his co-stars was that he was so often willing to shield them from blame for their mistakes. If an actor, no matter how small their part, fumbled a line or missed his cue, Grant might suddenly say he had forgotten his next line and ask for it to be given to him. By interceding this way, he deflected the potential wrath of the director toward the other actor. Co-stars and in particular leading ladies enjoyed working with him because he was a responsive actor, interacting with them in a scene rather than just saying his lines. He had an intuitive sense of using body language to bolster the words coming out of his mouth. He also had a keen sense of how to use the lighting on a set to an actor's best advantage and would often make suggestions for his female co-stars to help them better understand such technical aspects to their own benefit.

Of course, he could be a prima donna at times as well, particularly when he frustratingly felt he hadn't gotten a complete handle on his own character yet. Rather than take it out on any one particularly unlucky person, as certain other stars would, Grant would just fuss and fume, and then get over it and charm everyone again.

Undoubtedly there were times of frustration for him while making *The Howards of Virginia*. Over the course of filming (which was done both in Hollywood, as well as on location at the historical Colonial Williamsburg site in Virginia), Grant's instincts concluded that this would not be a very good film, which proved to be true. Although quite a few critics liked it (although often with reservations), its steep budget all but guaranteed it would lose money at the box office. Perhaps most vexing of all for Grant, because he was busy making this movie, he had to turn down an invitation from Alfred Hitchcock to star in *Foreign Correspondent* (1940), which proved to be a critical and commercial success.

●●●

I'll be yar now: *The Philadelphia Story*

Call it 'Kate's Revenge,' or 'Cary's Victory.' Either way, it was a triumph that proved to be a career milestone for just about everyone involved.

After the box office failure of *Holiday*, Katharine Hepburn mused that there probably was something after all to the charge that she was 'box office poison'. With no pending film commitments, she left Hollywood and went back East, where she sought to resume her Broadway career. Philip Barry, the author of *Holiday*, was a good friend of Hepburn's, and when he learned she was returning to the stage, he told her he had a new idea for a play that he thought she would be perfect for. Barry had been suffering through a string of flops in recent years, but he felt certain this new work would be the success he needed. His initial inspiration was Philadelphia socialite Helen Hope Montgomery Scott, but after spending time with Katharine and her family at their Connecticut home, it was the Hepburn clan themselves upon whom he based much about his characters.

His working title for the play was *Gentle Reader* (although Hepburn, in much of a need of a hit as Barry, would joke that it ought to be called *The Answer to This Maiden's Prayer*), and the premise was that a pair of magazine writers would spend a day at the home of the prestigious Lord family in order to cover the wedding of their eldest daughter, Tracy, who is set to marry George Kittredge, a self-made millionaire with political ambitions, who sees marrying Tracy as his entry into the upper strata of high society. In the course of their stay, the writers would uncover secrets that the ever-so-proper Lords would prefer to keep undisclosed. Additionally, Tracy finds herself romantically entangled between George, her ex-husband, C.K. Dexter Haven, who has come as a guest for the wedding, as well as one of the writers, Macaulay Connor. The underlying theme would be about privilege, and the loss of it, which is what excited Hepburn the most about the concept.

Barry refused to show Hepburn or anyone else what he had already written, but he did confess to her that he was having trouble deciding how the story would end in the third act. As the time grew closer to when they would have to start rehearsing the play, the actress repeatedly urged the playwright to get over his writer's block and finish the story. He finally did, but hardly to everyone's satisfaction. As the production went on the road to work out its kinks, Barry rewrote much of the third act.

Audiences had liked the play, now called *The Philadelphia Story* (1940), at preview performances in New Haven, Philadelphia, Baltimore, Washington, and Boston, and at last a New York opening was scheduled for March of 1939. Hepburn protested that the production still needed more work, and she urged a continuation of the preview tour, but the producers argued that avoiding Broadway much longer would send a signal that the play was troubled, and might doom it from the start in New York, which was all-important to any stage production's lasting success.

The New York theater critics loved the play, and it was an immediate smash hit, running for a solid year at the Shubert Theater on West 44th St. Much to her own astonishment, Katharine Hepburn found herself acclaimed as the toast of Broadway. Hollywood may have rejected her, but Manhattan loved her now.

Although she had ended her longtime romantic relationship with Howard Hughes in 1938, they remained friendly. When she told him she was going back to Broadway, he urged her to do a comedy, and what's more, to make certain she owned the film rights, so that she could parlay the play's success into a return to the movies. Then Hughes did one better than simply offering advice, and he purchased the film rights to *The Philadelphia Story* himself and gave them to Hepburn as a gift.

Proving that nothing succeeds like success, the Hollywood studios were all rabid to make a film version of the play. Warner Brothers thought it would make a great vehicle for Errol Flynn as Dexter Haven, perhaps with Ann Sheridan as Tracy, and Ronald Reagan for the part of Macaulay. Estimations by gossip columnists was that a studio bidding war for the play could drive the final price to well over $500,000.

Instead of entertaining offers however, Hepburn went straight to Louis B. Mayer at Metro-Goldwyn-Mayer, the most powerful studio in Hollywood. She offered MGM the coveted film rights for a mere $250,000, but with that came Hepburn in the lead role.

Additionally, she would have control over the choice of director and the rest of the cast. Mayer agreed.

Perhaps the mogul relished the opportunity to take a talented actress whom the other studios had deemed "washed up" and make her a star again. More likely he calculated that with the bargain price for the rights, and the fact that a film adaptation would not require a particularly large budget (indeed, ultimately it was made for under $1,000,000, which for MGM was small change), and with the right male stars alongside Hepburn, then . . . box office poison or not . . . there was almost no way that *The Philadelphia Story* could lose money for the studio.

The first, last, and only choice for Hepburn to direct was George Cukor. For her co-stars she requested MGM's two biggest names, Clark Gable and Spencer Tracy, but both were already signed to other productions. MGM suggested James Stewart for the role of Macaulay, and Hepburn agreed.

It was not quite as easy to cast the part of Dexter. MGM boasted that it had 'More Stars than there are in Heaven," but every top leading man they had under contract, such as Robert Montgomery, Fred Astaire, Robert Taylor, and William Powell, were either already committed to other films, or else were rejected by Hepburn as unsuited for the role. With the scheduled start of production looming and unwilling to incur the cost of postponing filming, Mayer told Hepburn she was free to look for an actor outside of MGM. That was all she needed to hear.

She turned to Grant. For him, this would be a moment of vindication. After three years of banishment from the majors, he would be invited to enter through the gate of the most major of them all, co-starring in one of the studio's most important films of the year.

Adding to this, Hepburn then had the pleasure of telling him that Mayer had told her she could spend up to $150,000 on the right actor, more money than Grant had ever earned for a single film before (Grant surprised and impressed many when he donated his salary for *The Philadelphia Story* to the British War Relief Society. It would not be the last time he would make such a gesture during World War II).

That was very welcome news, but Grant had one request: he must get top billing. This perhaps gave Hepburn pause, but if so, only for a moment. Giving up the top spot to Grant was a small sacrifice for her to make to secure his participation. Besides, contractually her name would also be above the title on the posters and newspaper advertisements, right alongside Grant's (and Jimmy Stewart would be joining them). She agreed ... and with that, Cary Grant was working for MGM[42]. The freelancer was in the very heart of the citadel of the studio contract system he had bucked.

Had Louis B. Mayer still been holding a grudge against the actor, he could have very easily nixed adding Grant to the film. No matter what Hepburn's contract promised about her having say over casting, MGM still held the purse strings, and the mogul could have simply rescinded the $150,000 offer and countered with, say, no more than a measly $10,000, take it or leave it. Of course, Grant would have refused such an insulting proposal, and that would be the end of it. While Mayer was a man who could carry a grudge far longer than most in Hollywood, he was also one of the shrewdest executives that the motion picture industry had ever seen. His cunning and relentlessness are what drove MGM to the top of the mountain in Hollywood and kept it there year after year. He could read the tea leaves as well as anyone, and better than most, and he saw a future for his studio in which Cary Grant had a place. Yes, Mayer and the other moguls had tried to barricade Grant from the upper tier of the business when he first struck off on his own, but that had accomplished nothing. Grant had gone on to make millions for Columbia and RKO. It was now only a matter of time before one of the majors finally brought him in from the cold, and if it was so inevitable, then why shouldn't it be MGM that reaped that bounty?

Cary Grant reported for work at MGM's Culver City studio on July the 5th of 1940.

---

42 To make *The Philadelphia Story*, Grant had to decline his second Alfred Hitchcock film in a row, *Mr. and Mrs. Smith*, a comedy co-starring Carole Lombard.

The Philadelphia Story had its premiere in New York City on the day after Christmas, but that was done only so that it officially qualified as a 1940 release for that year's Academy Awards. It did not go into widespread release around the U.S. until the third week in January 1941, by which point word of mouth ... and a flurry of laudatory reviews ... had built great anticipation for the film.

In its first four days showing in Manhattan, it set a new record for ticket sales at the cavernous Radio City Music Hall, with some 110,000 patrons braving wet and dismal winter weather to see it. It went on to set another record at Radio City by being held over for an unprecedented six weeks. All told, by the time the film finished its nationwide run in mid-1941, it had earned more than $3,000,000 in box office receipts.

When the Academy Awards nominations were announced, *The Philadelphia Story* was nominated for no fewer than six Oscars: Best Picture, George Cukor as Best Director, Katharine Hepburn as Best Actress, James Stewart as Best Supporting Actor, Ruth Hussey as Best Supporting Actress, and Donald Ogden Stewart for Best Screenplay[43]. The two Stewarts, Donald and Jimmy, won their categories.

It was much commented on that Grant was the only one of the four main actors to not receive a nomination. That would prove to be typical for much of the rest of his career.

❊❊❊

As 1940 drew to a close and the new year was about to dawn, Cary Grant was in a very different position from just four years before. He had begun the journey by leaping into an abyss, relinquishing the security of a studio contract for the uncertainty of

---

43 Philip Barry had initially been considered by MGM to adapt his play for the screen, but the studio felt he was asking far too large of a salary, so instead they turned to Barry's old friend, Stewart. Uncredited as a co-screenwriter was the film's producer, Joseph L. Mankiewicz, who did much to tighten up the original story, including eliminating the character of Tracy Lord's brother, whom Mankiewicz deemed superfluous. He also built up the role of C.K. Dexter Haven once Grant was added to the cast, and wrote a dialogue-free opening segment, which portrayed the dissolution of Dexter and Tracy's marriage in quasi-screwball style.

charting his own course. He found an industry that in some parts was hostile to him, and actively rooting for his failure.

Along the way he found many more individuals who were happy to help him, and who cheered every time he climbed another rung of the ladder. Over the course of those four years, he had gone from second-rank leading man to being an indisputable A-level star, culminating in headlining one of the biggest box office smashes of the year for the most dominant studio in Hollywood.

It was not without cost to him, particularly personally. However, the boy who had been Archie Leach, who had put Bristol and its sorrows behind him, had learned through hard-won experience just how to beat the formidable odds arrayed against him. He was more than a survivor; he was a creator, and he set about creating a new existence for himself in America. Once that was done, he went to work crafting an even greater and more lasting legacy. He made himself a legend.

Later in his life he poetically remarked, "I wanted to be somebody I wanted to be until finally I became that person. Or he became me."

The years from 1937 to 1940 were the fires in which he forged that somebody.

FREELANCE FILMS 1937-1940

TOPPER
Released July 16, 1937
Tagline: "90 ROARING MINUTES OF LAUGHS!"

Produced by Milton H. Bren for Hal Roach Studio
Distributed by Metro-Goldwyn-Mayer

Directed by Norman Z. McLeod
Screenplay by Jack Jerne, Eric Hatch, Eddie Moran
From a novel by Thorne Smith
Cinematography by Norbert Brodine
Photographic Effects by Roy Seawright
Music by Marvin Hatley (with Hoagy Carmichael)
Constance Bennett as Marion Kerby
Cary Grant as George Kerby
Roland Young as Cosmo Topper
Billie Burke as Clara Topper
Alan Mowbray as Wilkins
Eugene Pallette as Casey
Arthur Lake as the Elevator Boy
Hedda Hopper as Mrs. Stuyvesant
Hoagy Carmichael as Hoagy
Vince Degan, Mack McLean, Bill Seckler and Martha Tilton as
 Three Hits and a Miss

"The giddy rigamarole is for those who can take their death ribald and their fantasy straight. Constance Bennett and Cary Grant are suitable as Kerbys. But it is Roland Young's show. Between the capricious antics of his abstract companions and the carping of Billie Burke as his wife, his talent for being harassed finds exquisite expression." – *Literary Digest*

THE AWFUL TRUTH
Released October 21, 1937
Tagline: "THE YEAR'S FUNNIEST, SUNNIEST, HONEYEST COMEDY!"

Produced by Leo McCarey and Everett Riskin for Columbia Pictures

Directed by Leo McCarey
Screenplay by Viña Delmar with Sidney Buchman and Leo McCarey (uncredited)
From a play by Arthur Richman
Cinematography by Joseph Walker
Music by Morris Stoloff

Irene Dunne as Lucy Warriner
Cary Grant as Jerry Warriner
Ralph Bellamy as Daniel Leeson
Alexander D'Arcy as Armand Duvalle
Cecil Cunningham as Aunt Patsy
Marguerite Churchill as Barbara Vance
Joyce Compton as Dixie Belle Lee
George C. Pearce as 'Dad'
Miki Morita as Armand's Butler
Skippy as Mr. Smith

"To be frank, *The Awful Truth* is awfully unimportant, but it is also one of the more laughable screen comedies of 1937, a fairly good vintage year. Its comedy is almost purely physical – like that of the old Avery Hopwood stage farces – with only here and there a lone gag to interrupt the pure poetry of motion, yet its unapologetic return to the fundamentals of comedy seems, we repeat, original and daring." – Bosley Crowther, *New York Times*

BRINGING UP BABY
Released February 18, 1938
Tagline: "IT'S A DOWNPOUR OF UPROAR!"
Produced by Howard Hawks and Cliff Reid for RKO Radio Pictures

Directed by Howard Hawks
Screenplay by Dudley Nichols and Hagar Wilde with Howard Hawks (uncredited)
From a story by Hagar Wilde
Cinematography by Russell Metty
Music by Roy Webb

Katharine Hepburn as Susan Vance
Cary Grant as David Huxley
Charles Ruggles as Major Horace Applegate
Walter Catlett as Slocum
Barry Fitzgerald as Mr. Gogarty
Fritz Feld as Dr. Lehmann
Virginia Walker as Alice Swallow
Skippy as George
Neissa as Baby

"Without peradventure of a doubt, *Bringing Up Baby* will take its place among the most insane comedies of the year, and yet one of the most original, and fantastically amusing. It's incidentally an absorbing event. Never a dull moment. And you can't tell what's going to happen next. Miss Hepburn does a difficult role with great ability and is matched in skill by Grant. These two carry the picture." – *Los Angeles Times*

HOLIDAY
Released June 15, 1938
Tagline: "EVERY DAY'S A HOLIDAY...WHEN YOU'RE IN LOVE!"

Produced by Everett Riskin for Columbia Pictures

Directed by George Cukor
Screenplay by Donald Ogden Stewart and Sidney Buchman
From a play by Philip Barry
Cinematography by Franz Planer
Music by Morris Stoloff

Katharine Hepburn as Linda Seton
Cary Grant as Johnny Case
Doris Nolan as Julia Seton
Lew Ayers as Ned Seaton
Edward Everett Horton as Nick Potter
Jean Dixon as Susan Potter
Henry Kolker as Edward Seton
Henry Daniell as Seton Cram
Binnie Barnes as Laura Cram

"That sweet, canary bird replete, pussy cat smile to be observed on the faces of Columbia executives is quite likely inspired by Katharine Hepburn's work in *Holiday*. For it is her perfect answer to 'independents' who, a short time ago, dared to class her as a 'has been'. Never has Hepburn given a more brilliant performance; never a more human one. Cary Grant is thoroughly at home, and most appealing as Johnny." – Mae Tinée, *Chicago Daily Tribune*

GUNGA DIN
Released February 17, 1939
Tagline: "THRILLS FOR A THOUSAND MOVIES PLUNDERED FOR ONE MIGHTY SHOW!"

Produced by George Stevens for RKO Radio Pictures

Directed by George Stevens
Screenplay by Joel Sayre and Fred Guiol with Ben Hecht and Charles MacArthur

From stories by Rudyard Kipling
Cinematography by John H. August
Music by Alfred Newman

Cary Grant as Sgt. Archibald Cutter
Victor McLaglen as Sgt. "Mac" MacChesney
Douglas Fairbanks, Jr. as Sgt. Thomas Ballantine
Sam Jaffe as Gunga Din
Eduardo Ciannelli as Guru
Joan Fontaine as Emaline Stebbins
Montagu Love as Col. Weed
Robert Coote as Sgt. Higginbotham
Abner Biberman as Chota
Annie as Annie

"With a poet in the credit lines, it is hardly surprising that *Gunga Din* should turn about to be as jaunty as a Barrack Room Ballad, as splendid as a Durbar, as exciting and at times as preposterous as a Pearl White serial. Thanks to the collaboration of the late Mr. Kipling, who wrote for the cinema without knowing it, it moves with all the discipline, dash and color of a vanished time, when Mr. Disraeli was Prime Minister and the empire had a good conscience. Although its mid portions tend to sag a bit under the weight of Victorian destiny, it blossoms at both ends into sequences of magnificently explosive action." – Bosley Crowther, *New York Times*

ONLY ANGELS HAVE WINGS
Released May 25, 1939
Tagline: "EACH DAY A RENDEZVOUS WITH PERIL… EACH NIGHT A MEETING WITH ROMANCE!"

Produced by Howard Hawks for Columbia Pictures

Directed by Howard Hawks
Screenplay by Jules Furthman with Howard Hawks (uncredited)
From a story by Anne Wigton

Cinematography by Joseph Walker
Music by Morris Stoloff

Cary Grant as Geoff Carter
Jean Arthur as Bonnie Lee
Richard Barthelmess as Bat McPherson
Rita Hayworth as Judy McPherson
Thomas Mitchell as Kid Dabb
Sig Rumann as Dutchy
Allyn Joslyn as Les Peters
Donald Berry as Tex Gordon
Victor Kilian as Sparks
John Carroll as Gent Shelton
Noah Berry, Jr. as Joe Souther

"Columbia has a winner. Story has substance, movement, romance. Every facet of *Only Angels Have Wings* is big league. The Grant-Arthur cynicism and unyielding romantics are kept at a high standard. Thomas Mitchell's devoted aide is never permitted to become banal, and there are opportunities in plenty where it might so have been. Rita Hayworth as Barthelmess' wife is likewise impressive. She's a good-looking gal with an ah-voom chassis." – Abel Green, *Variety*

IN NAME ONLY
Released August 18, 1939
Tagline: "MARRIAGE VS. ROMANCE! MUST IT BE THAT WAY?"

Produced by George Haight for RKO Radio Pictures

Directed by John Cromwell
Screenplay by Richard Sherman
From a novel by Bessie Breuer
Cinematography by J. Roy Hunt
Music by Roy Webb

Carole Lombard as Julie Eden
Cary Grant as Alec Walker
Kay Francis as Maida Walker
Charles Coburn as Mr. Walker
Helen Vinson as Suzanne Duross
Jonathan Hale as Dr. Gateson
Peggy Ann Garner as Ellen
Maurice Moscovich as Dr. Muller

"This is a well-made depressing little picture of unhappy marriage. It is often sentimental, but the general impression which remains is quite an authentic one – a glossy photographic likeness of gloom: fruitless discussions about Reno, polite chicanery over the long-distance 'phone, hate in a sherry glass, the rattled nerve and the despair of any day being different from today." - Graham Greene, *The Spectator*

HIS GIRL FRIDAY
Released January 18, 1940
Tagline: "SHE LEARNED ABOUT MEN FROM HIM!"

Produced by Howard Hawks for Columbia Pictures

Directed by Howard Hawks
Screenplay by Charles Lederer with Howard Hawks and Ben Hecht (uncredited)
From a play by Ben Hecht and Charles MacArthur
Cinematography by Joseph Walker
Music by Morris Stoloff

Cary Grant as Walter Burns
Rosalind Russell as Hildy Johnson
Ralph Bellamy as Bruce Baldwin
Gene Lockhart as Sheriff Hartwell
Clarence Kolb as the Mayor
Abner Biberman as Diamond Louie

John Qualen as Earl Williams
Helen Mack as Mollie Malloy
Alma Kruger as Mrs. Baldwin
Billy Gilbert as Joe Pettibone

"Hysteria is one of the communicable diseases and *His Girl Friday* is a more pernicious carrier than Typhoid Mary. It takes you by the scruff of the neck in the first reel and it shakes you madly, bellowing hoarsely the while, for the remaining six or seven. Charles Lederer, who wrote the adaptation, has transported it so brilliantly it is hard to believe that Hecht and MacArthur were not thinking of Rosalind Russell, or someone equally high-heeled, when they wrote about the Hildy Johnson who once had a printer's ink transfusion from a Machiavellian managing editor and never again could qualify as a normal human being. Under Howard Hawks' direction, the cast has acknowledged the clamoring script with performances that are hard, brittle and strained to the breaking point, if not somewhat beyond, as though they were waiting for the camera to look the other way so they could collapse with honor." – Frank S. Nugent, *New York Times*

MY FAVORITE WIFE
Released May 17, 1940
Tagline: KISS AND RUN CARY CAUGHT BETWEEN TWO BLUSHING BRIDES!"

Produced by Leo McCarey for RKO Radio Pictures

Directed by Garson Kanin and Leo McCarey (uncredited)
Screenplay by Bella Spewack and Sam Spewack with Leo McCarey, Garson Kanin and John McClain (uncredited)
From a story by Leo McCarey
Cinematography by Rudolph Maté
Music by Roy Webb

Irene Dunne as Ellen Arden
Cary Grant as Nick Dunne
Randolph Scott as Stephen Burkett
Gail Patrick as Bianca Bates Arden
Ann Shoemaker as Ma Wagstaff
Scotty Beckett as Tim Arden
Mary Lou Harrington as Chinch Arden
Granville Bates as Judge Bryson
Pedro de Cordoba as Dr. Kohlmar

"There is some of the best comedy work in *My Favorite Wife*, a sort of nonsense-sequel to *The Awful Truth*. There is also some of the worst plot-making…apart from it being quite impossible, which may be called comic license, it forces its best people to treat each other with an aimless viciousness that even Boris Karloff might hesitate to reveal to his public. Most of the characters can manage to cover up this bankruptcy of motivation with quips and tumbles. In addition, it shows Cary Grant developing a very pleasant style of male-animal humor, with charm and a distinct sense of where to poise or throw his weight." – Otis Ferguson, *The New Republic*

THE HOWARDS OF VIRGINIA
Released September 19, 1940
Tagline: "THE VIVID DRAMA OF A NATION'S BIRTH!"

Produced by Frank Lloyd and Jack H. Skirball for Columbia Pictures

Directed by Frank Lloyd
Screenplay by Sidney Buchman
From a novel by Elizabeth Page
Cinematography by Bert Glennon
Music by Richard Hageman

Cary Grant as Matt Howard
Martha Scott as Jane Peyton Howard

Sir Cedric Hardwicke as Fleetwood Peyton
Alan Marshal as Roger Peyton
Richard Carlson as Thomas Jefferson
Paul Kelly as Captain Jabez Allen
Richard Gaines as Patrick Henry
George Houston as George Washington
Dickie Jones as young Matt Howard

"Columbia…seems to have tackled a larger canvas than it could paint effectively, with the result that this cavalcade of Colonial and Revolutionary America, while ambitious, expensive, and generally interesting, comes to life all too infrequently. Obviously miscast, Cary Grant meets the exigencies of a difficult role with more gusto than persuasion." – *Newsweek*

THE PHILADELPHIA STORY
Released December 26, 1940
Tagline: "THE 3-STAR LAUGH HIT!"

Produced by Joseph L. Mankiewicz for Metro-Goldwyn-Mayer

Directed by George Cukor
Written by Donald Ogden Stewart with Joseph L. Mankiewicz and Waldo Salt (uncredited)
From a play by Philip Barry
Cinematography by Joseph Ruttenberg
Music by Franz Waxman

Cary Grant as C.K. Dexter Haven
Katharine Hepburn as Tracy Lord
James Stewart as Macauley Connor
Ruth Hussey as Elizabeth Imbrie
John Howard as George Kittredge
Roland Young as Uncle Willie
John Halliday as Seth Lord
Mary Nash as Margaret Lord
Virginia Weidler as Dinah Lord

Henry Daniell as Sidney Kidd

"All those folks who wrote Santa Claus asking him to send them a sleek new custom-built comedy with fast lines and the very finest in Hollywood fittings got their wish just one day late with the opening of *The Philadelphia Story* yesterday at the Music Hall. For this present, which really comes via Metro-Goldwyn-Mayer, has just about everything that a blue-chip comedy should have – a witty, romantic script derived by Donald Ogden Stewart out of Philip Barry's successful play; the flavor of high-society elegance, in which the patrons invariably luxuriate, and a splendid cast of performers headed by Katharine Hepburn, James Stewart and Cary Grant. If it doesn't play out this year and well into next they should turn the Music Hall into a shooting gallery." – Bosley Crowther, *New York Times*

RADIO APPEARANCES 1937-1940

Lux Radio Theatre
3/18/1937
CBS
"Madame Butterfly" costarring Grace Moore

Lux Radio Theatre
6/13/1938
CBS
"Theodora Goes Wild" costarring Irene Dunne

Silver Theatre
10/16/1938
CBS
"Wings in the Dark" costarring Phyllis Brooks

The Circle
NBC
Intermittently co-hosted this weekly roundtable series from January to June, 1939

Screen Guild Theatre
CBS
4/30/1939
"Alone in Paris" costarring Irene Dunne

Lux Radio Theatre
5/29/1939
CBS
"Only Angels Have Wings" costarring Jean Arthur

Hollywood British Film Colony Broadcast
NBC
6/11/1939
Grant joined other British Commonwealth subjects working in Hollywood, including Ronald Colman, Errol Flynn and Vivien Leigh, to honor King George VI and Queen Elizabeth as they visited the United States.

Lux Radio Theatre
9/11/1939
CBS
"The Awful Truth" costarring Claudette Colbert

Screen Guild Theatre
CBS
9/24/1939
Special appearance to promote the Motion Picture Relief Fund

Lux Radio Theatre
12/11/1939
CBS
"In Name Only" costarring Carole Lombard and Kay Francis

INDEX

A Woman Rebels, 69
Aherne, Brian, v, vi
Air Circus, The, 133
Alice Adams, 21
An Affair to Remember, 134
Angels With Dirty Faces, 119
Annie Oakley, 121
Arden, Eve, 77
Arlen, Richard, 21, 30
Arthur, Jean, 134, 138-139, 149, 158, 178, 184
Astaire, Fred, 30, 48, 64, 120, 169
Ayers, Lew, 30, 81, 176
Bachelor Mother, 139
Ball, Lucille, 77
Barry, Philip, 79-80, 167, 171, 176, 182-183
Barthelmess, Richard, 135, 139, 178
Bass, Mabel Johnson, 3
Bellamy, Ralph, 49, 56, 61, 110, 149, 151, 153, 174, 179
Bennett, Constance, 35, 41, 80, 173
Bennett, Joan, 20
Berman, Pandro S., 63, 121, 125
Berry, Noah Jr., 136, 178
Biberman, Abner, 121, 152, 177, 179
Big Brown Eyes, 20
Blonde Venus, 18, 88
Blondell, Joan, 138
Boom Boom, 12
Boyer, Charles, 134, 145
Brandt, Harry, 69
Breuer, Bessie, 140, 178

Brian, Mary, 24-25
Bringing Up Baby, 64, 69-70, 75, 77-78, 80, 82, 85, 100, 120, 130, 138, 175
Brisson, Carl, 155
Brisson, Freddie, 155-156, 161
Brooks, Phyllis, 24-25, 65, 85-87, 107, 124, 130, 133, 143-144, 156-157, 161, 184
Broadway Melody, 12
Buchman, Sidney, 80, 83, 164, 174, 176, 181-182
Buchner, Jr., William P., 87
Buencamino, Felipe, 87
Cagney, James, 27, 61
Capra, Frank, 32, 45-47, 49, 62, 94, 122, 134
Catlett, Walter, 71, 175
Ceiling Zero, 69, 133
Celeste, Olga, 76
Chamberlain, Neville, 129
Chang, Anna, 13
Chaplin, Charlie, 4, 23-24, 70
Charig, Phil, 14
Cherrill, Virginia, 23-25, 66, 107
Child-Villiers, George, 24
Churchill, Winston, 129, 146
Circle, The, 131-132, 184
City Lights, 23
Cleopatra, 19
Coburn, Charles, 142, 179
Cohn, Harry, 45-47, 49-52, 61, 79-80, 94-95, 133-135, 147-150, 153, 158, 163-165
Colbert, Claudette, 20-21, 27, 45, 131, 149, 185

Colman, Ronald, 87, 131-132, 185
Come On, Marines!, 121
Comingore, Dorothy, 135
Cooper, Bobby, 24
Cooper, Gary, 16, 18, 21, 26-27, 66
Cooper, Merian C., 63
Coote, Robert, 121, 145, 177
Count of Monte Cristo, The, 126
Coward, Noel, 84, 132
Crawford, Joan, v, 69, 149
Cromwell, John, 142, 178
Crosby, Bing, 27
Cukor, George, 19-20, 79-80, 83, 85, 169, 171, 176, 182
Damita, Lili, 16
Dawn Patrol, The, 69, 133, 135
DeMille, Cecil B., 131
Destination Tokyo, 146
Dietrich, Marlene, v, 19, 25, 27, 69, 87-88
Dillingham, Charles, 9
Dixon, Jean, 82, 176
Douglas, Melvyn, 30, 158
Dracula, 24
Drums Along the Mohawk, 163
Dumas, Alexandre, 102, 120, 126, 130
Dunne, Irene, 11, 48-49, 51-53, 56-57, 61, 64, 79, 97, 108, 111-112, 131, 134, 149, 157-158, 160, 174, 180, 184
duPont, Marion, 68-69, 162
Eagle and the Hawk, The, 19, 140
Edington, Harry E., 25-26
Enoch Arden, 158, 160
Enter Madame, 19
Fairbanks, Douglas, 9, 124
Fairbanks, Douglas Jr., 25, 64, 122-124, 177
Father Goose, 62, 146
Faulkner, William, 118

Ferber, Edna, 77
Fields, Gracie, 87
Fields, W.C., 34-35, 157
Flynn, Errol, 161, 168, 185
Fonda, Henry, 70
Fontaine, Joan, 122, 125, 177
Ford, John, 24, 134
Foreign Correspondent, 166
Fowler, Gene, 148, 157
Francis, Kay, 140, 142, 179, 185
Frankenstein, 24
Front Page, The, 118, 120, 147-149
Furness, Betty, 24
Furthman, Jules, 133, 177
Gable, Clark, 20, 27, 42, 45, 61, 120, 140, 169
Garner, Peggy Ann, 142, 179
Garbo, Greta, 25, 69
Gering, Marion, 15, 125
Gilded Lily, The, 21
Gish, Lillian, 14
Golden Dawn, 11
Goldstein, Robert, 164
Goldwyn, Samuel, 26, 121
Gone With the Wind, 56, 59, 85, 121, 148, 163-164
Good Times, 9-10
Grady, Billy, 15
Grant, Cary
   Accent, 11
   Arrives in Hollywood, 14
   Arrives in U.S., 9
   Begins dating Phyllis Brooks, 24
   Birth, 2
   Childhood, 2-8
   Death, v
   Father, *see Leach, Elias*
   Goes independent, 28
   Joins Pender Troup, 6
   Marriage and Divorce, *see Cherrill, Virginia*

Mother, *see Leach, Elsie*
Name Change, 16
Signs with Columbia, 30
Signs with Paramount, 16
Signs with RKO, 32
And World War II, 145-146, 169
Guiol, Fred, 121, 125, 176
Gunga Din, 101-102, 118-122, 125-130, 139, 147, 152, 176-177
Hale, Jonathan, 142, 179
Hamilton, Neil, 21
Hammerstein, Arthur, 11
Hands Across the Table, 21
Hanneford Family, 9
Hardwicke, Cedric, 145, 181
Harlow, Jean, 21, 34
Hathaway, Henry, 20
von Haugwitz-Reventlow, Kurt, 161
Having Wonderful Time, 122
Hawks, Howard, 69-70, 78, 89, 98, 103, 109, 118, 133-134, 136, 147, 150, 163, 175, 177, 179-180
Hayworth, Rita, 135-136, 139, 178
Hearst, William Randolph, 14, 16, 65
Hecht, Ben, 118-122, 126, 147-149, 176, 179-180
Hellinger, Mark, 153
Hepburn, Katharine, v, 19, 21, 64, 69-71, 74-82, 84-85, 98, 100, 120, 135, 140, 167-171, 175-176, 178, 183
Herzbrun, Walter, 15
His Girl Friday, 110, 147, 153-154, 156-157, 179
Hitchcock, Alfred, 30, 166, 170
Hitler, Adolf, 129, 145
Hively, George, 77

Holiday (play), 79, 167
Holiday (1930 version)
Holiday (1938 version), 83, 85, 100, 130, 135, 164, 167, 175-176
Hopkins, Miriam, 64, 87
Horton, Edward Everett, 80, 82, 176
Hot Saturday, 66, 159
Howards of Virginia, The, 114, 163-166, 181
Howard, Leslie, 69-70
Hughes, Howard, 70, 147, 161, 168
Hussey, Ruth, 171, 182
Hutton, Barbara, 161-163, 165
I'm No Angel, 19
In Name Only, 104, 139-140, 142-143, 178, 185
Informer, The, 64, 121
Irving, Washington, 158
Iturbi, José, 132
Jackson, Joe, 9
Jaffe, Sam, 122, 124, 177
Joy of Living, 122
Kanin, Garson, 122, 156, 180
Karloff, Boris, 132, 181
Karns, Roscoe, 149
Kaufman, George S., 77
Keaton, Buster, 70
Keith, Nancy "Slim", 147
Kelly, Jack (Orry-Kelly), 10
Kennedy, John F., 143
Kerr, Deborah, 134
Kipling, Rudyard, 102, 118-119, 121-122, 128, 130, 177
Kiss and Make-Up, 19
Korda, Alexander, 34, 122, 146
La Chienne, 88
Ladies and Gentlemen, 119, 148
Ladies Should Listen, 19
Lampe, Robert, 26

Lamour, Dorothy, 163
Landi, Elissa, 24
Landis, Carole, 163
Langham, Ria, 140
Last Flight, The, 135
Laughton, Charles, 44
Leach, Archie, *see Cary Grant*
Leach, Elias, 2-3, 6-8, 22, 23
Leach, Elsie, 2-3, 22-23, 65, 86, 130, 143-144, 146
Leach, John, 2-3
Lederer, Charles, 148, 180
Leisen, Mitchell, 21, 134
Libaire, Dorothy, 15
Lives of a Bengal Lancer, The, 19
Lloyd, Frank, 165, 181
Lloyd, Harold, 32, 44, 50, 70, 99
Lloyd, Marie, 88
Lockhart, Gene, 149, 179
Lombard, Carole, 19, 27, 104, 131, 140, 149, 170, 179, 185
Lost Horizon, 32, 45-46, 61, 94, 122, 163
Lothian, Philip Henry Kerr (Lord), 145, 165
Love Affair, 134, 139
Lubitsch, Ernst, 20
Lucky to Me, 143
Lux Radio Theatre, The, 131, 139, 184-185
MacArthur, Charles, 118, 147-148, 176, 179-180
MacDonald, Jeanette, 12
MacDonald, Torbert, 143
MacMurray, Fred, 21, 158
McClain, John, 159, 180
McCrea, Joel, 25
McLaglen, Victor, 121, 124, 177
Man Who Reclaimed His Head, The, 24
Marceline, 9
March, Fredric, 19, 70
Mark of Zorro, The, 124
Marx, Chico, 132
Marx, Groucho, 131-132
Mary of Scotland, 69
Maugham, W. Somerset, 158
Mayer, Louis B., 168, 170
Memory of Love, 140
Menjou, Adolphe, 77
Milestone, Lewis, 147
Miller, Ann, 77
Mr. Smith Goes to Washington, 121
Mitchell, Thomas, 136
Montgomery, Robert, 70
Morris, Chester, 21
Mother Carey's Chickens, 78
Mutiny on the Bounty, 20, 165
My Favorite Wife, 157-158, 161, 180-181
Neagle, Anne, 88
Neale, L. Wright, 26
Nichols, Dudley, 69, 120, 175
Nikki, 13-14, 16, 135
Niven, David, 139, 145, 161
Nolan, Doris, 80, 176
Northwest Passage, 163
Nothing Sacred, 119
Nugent, Frank S., 77, 180
Oakie, Jack, 119, 122
O'Brian, Pat, 147
Olivier, Laurence, 145
Once Upon a Honeymoon, 146
Only Angels Have Wings, 133-134, 138-140, 147, 177-178
Page, Elizabeth, 163, 181
Patrick, Gail, 158, 160, 181
Pender, Bob, 6, 8-10
Pender, Margaret, 6, 8
Philadelphia Story, The (play), 168
Philadelphia Story, The (film), 167, 169, 170-171, 182-183

Pickford, Mary, 9
Powell, William, 42, 62, 169
Price, Vincent, 11
Prisoner of Zenda, The, 122
Quality Street, 69
Raines, Claude, 24
Rathbone, Basil, 132, 145
Reagan, Ronald, 168
Renoir, Jean, 88
Reventlow, Lance, 161
Rice, Grantland, 132
Rip Van Winkle, 158
Robinson, Casey, 13
Robinson, Edward G., 14, 25, 88
Robson, May, 73
Rogers, Ginger, 48, 64, 77, 120, 139, 148-149
Roland, Gilbert, 41, 161
Ruggles, Charles, 16, 175
Ruggles, Wesley, 21, 158
Rumann, Sig, 136, 178
Russell, Rosalind, 109, 150, 154-156, 179-180
Ryskind, Morrie, 36, 152
Sabu, 122
Sanders, George, 122
Saunders, John Monk, 13-14, 135
Sayre, Joel, 121-123, 176
Scarlet Street, 88
Schenck, Joseph, 87
Schulberg, B.P., 15-16, 30
Scott, Helen Hope Montgomery, 167
Scott, Martha, 181
Scott, Randolph, 31, 66, 67-69, 106, 159, 162, 181
Selznick, David O., 80, 85, 121-122
She Done Him Wrong, 19
Sheffield, Reginald, 128
Sheridan, Ann, 168
Sherman, Richard, 140
Shubert, J.J., 12
Shubert, Lee, 12
Singapore Sue, 14-15
Small, Edward, 29, 118
Spewack, Bella, 158, 180
Spewack, Samuel, 158, 180
Spirit of '76, The, 164
Stage Door, 77, 80
Stalin, Josef, 145
Stanwyck, Barbara, 138
Steiller, Daisy, 130-131
Stevens, George, 21, 120-121, 125, 176
Stewart, Donald Ogden, 80, 119, 171, 176, 182-183
Stewart, James, 169-171, 183
Story, Belle, 9
Street Singer, The, 12
Sullivan, Ed, 34
Suzy, 21
Sylvia Scarlett, v, 19, 69
Talmadge, Norma, 66
Taylor, Robert, 169
Tennyson, Alfred (Lord), 158
Theodora Goes Wild, 48, 131, 184
Thief of Bagdad, The, 124
This is the Night, 16
Three Musketeers, The (novel), 102, 120, 126
Three Musketeers, The (film), 124
Tree of Liberty, The, 163
Todd, Thelma, 16
Tone, Franchot, 21
Too Many Husbands, 158, 160
Tracy, Spencer, 169
Vincent, Frank W., 25-28, 30, 70, 155, 165
Viva Villa!, 133
Walker, Virginia, 72, 175
Walsh, Raoul, 20

Warner, Jack, 63, 87
West, Mae, 19, 27
Wheeler, Bert, 120
Wigton, Anne, 133, 177
Wilcox, Herbert, 88, 145
Wilde, Hager, 69, 175
Williams, Hope, 79
Wizard of Oz, The, 121
Women, The, 150, 155
Wonderful Night, The, 12
Woolsey, Robert, 120
Wray, Fay, 13-14, 16
Wuthering Heights, 121, 148
Young, Loretta, 87
Young, Roland, 16, 35, 49, 173, 182
Ziegfeld, Florenz, 11

www.ingramcontent.com/pod-product-compliance
Lightning Source LLC
Chambersburg PA
CBHW051055160426
43193CB00010B/1191